KU-728-661

THE SIMPSONS™
HANDBOOK

SECRET
TIPS FROM
THE PROS

The Simpsons™, created by Matt Groening, is the copyrighted and trademarked property
of Twentieth Century Fox Film Corporation. Used with permission. All rights reserved.

THE SIMPSONS™ HANDBOOK: SECRET TIPS FROM THE PROS

Copyright © 2007 by

Matt Groening Productions, Inc. All rights reserved.

No part of this book may be used or reproduced in any manner whatsoever without written permission
except in the case of brief quotations embodied in critical articles and reviews.

HarperCollins*Publishers*
77–85 Fulham Palace Road, Hammersmith, London W6 8JB
www.harpercollins.co.uk
Published by HARPER 2007
1 3 5 7 9 8 6 4 2
ISBN-13   978-0-00-725494-1
ISBN-10   0-00-725494-6
Printed in China

Publisher: Matt Groening
Creative Director: Bill Morrison
Managing Editor: Terry Delegeane
Director of Operations: Robert Zaugh
Art Director: Nathan Kane
Special Projects Art Director: Serban Cristescu
Production Manager: Christopher Ungar
Production/Design: Karen Bates, Nathan Hamill, Art Villanueva
Staff Artists: Chia-Hsien Jason Ho, Mike Rote
Administration: Sherri Smith
Legal Guardian: Susan A. Grode

THE SIMPSONS™ HANDBOOK: SECRET TIPS FROM THE PROS

Edited by Bill Morrison

Book Design and Art Direction by Serban Cristescu

Character Art by
Kevin M. Newman with Mike B. Anderson, Norman Auble, Darrel Bowen,
Shaun Cashman, Liz Climo, Jonathan Gebhart, Chia-Hsien Jason Ho, Nathan Kane, Bill Morrison,
Rob Oliver, Julius Preite, Edward Rosas, Mike Rote, Erick Tran, Joe Wack, Paul Wee

Background and Prop Art by Lance Wilder

HarperCollins Editors: Hope Innelli, Jeremy Cesarec

Special Thanks to:
Karen Bates, Pete Benson, N. Vyolet Diaz, Deanna MacLellan, Mili Smythe, and Ursula Wendel

THE SIMPSONS™
HANDBOOK

SECRET TIPS FROM THE PROS

HARPER

NEW YORK · LONDON · TORONTO · SYDNEY

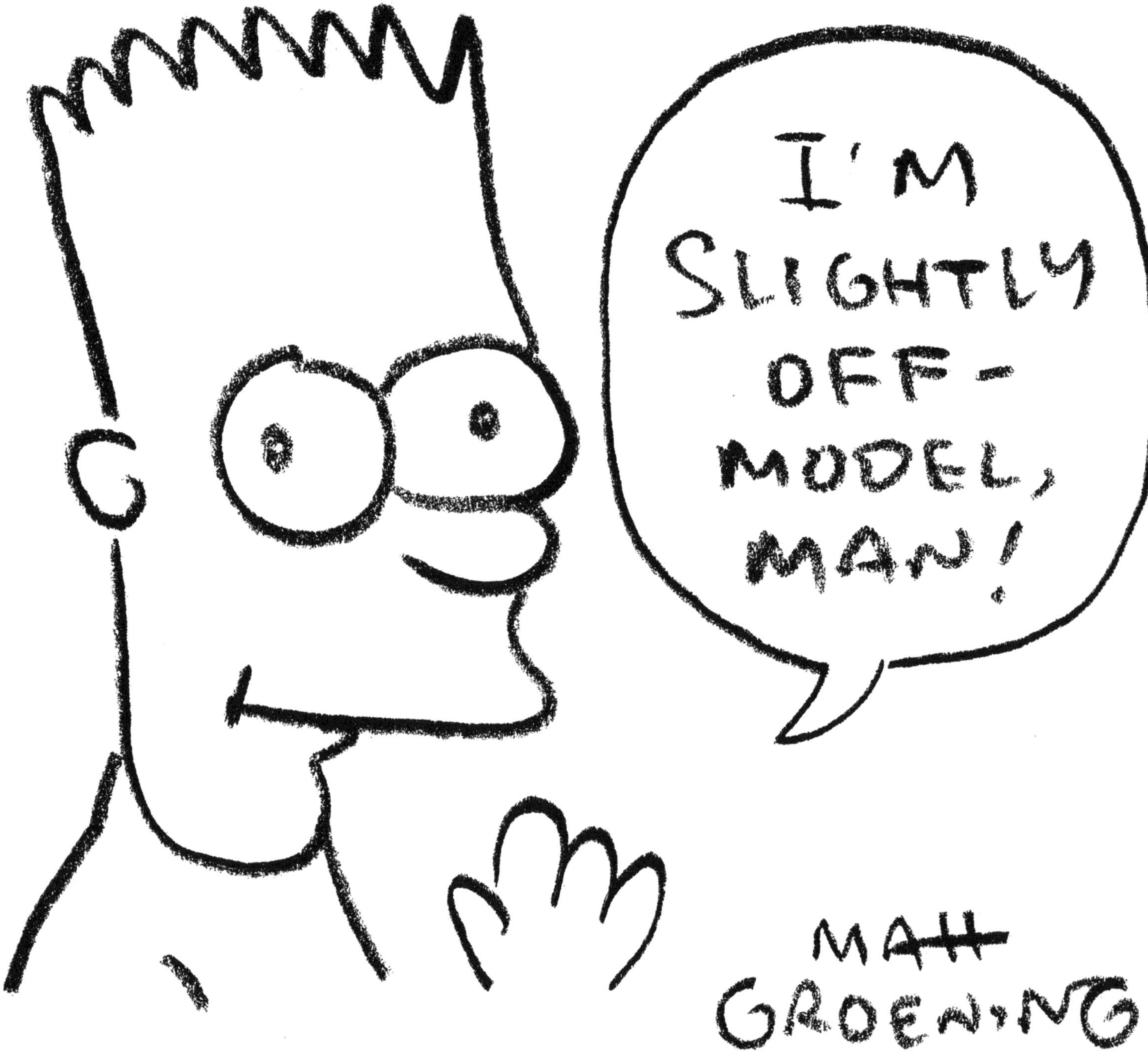
I'M SLIGHTLY OFF-MODEL, MAN!
MATT GROENING

BULGY EYEBALLS AND FREAKISH OVERBITES: AN INTRODUCTION

've been a drawer of curves and ovals and squiggly lines for about as long as I can remember. I can even pinpoint the moment when my fate as a lifelong compulsive doodler was sealed: the first day of the first grade. That's when I began to draw, and draw and draw and draw, on whatever surface and with whatever tool I had handy. Why? Because I found school so unbelievably boring that I had to do something—anything—to keep myself from going out of my mind.

Eventually, those crude grade-school scribbles grew more polished and refined, resulting in that crude grown-up cartoon powerhouse we all love and worship, "The Simpsons." And today, "The Simpsons" remains part of a special but disappearing art form: two-dimensional hand-drawn animation, with heavy emphasis on large heads, beard lines, and comical flab.

Back in 1993, we put together *Cartooning with the Simpsons*, the inspiration for this monumental instructional art tome. But as great as the original work was, it looks like a bootleg coloring book for little babies compared to this big ol' brick. Check out the gatefolds and tracing paper overlays, the oodles and oodles of Simpsons characters, including Milhouse, and the highly professional tips and tricks from the animators who have toiled on the show till they have weird little skin grooves where they hold their pencils. I assure you that if you practice hard and long enough, you too can develop your own special little skin grooves.

I've got lots of cartooning advice, if you can stop drawing for a second and pay attention: Keep things simple. (You can convey space, motion, and feeling with surprisingly few lines.) Save your stuff. (Don't let your mom or stepmom throw it out.) Always finish what you're working on. (There's nothing like completing a full story.) Go ahead and copy other styles. (But don't just stick to one.) Check out the original artwork of cartoonists and artists you dig. (Pros do make mistakes, but you have to see the originals to learn how they fixed them.) And finally (here's the tough one): Be original! (Keep practicing, develop your own style, and try to surprise yourself.)

This book is full of rules about how to draw the Simpsons characters, and those rules have made it possible for thousands of artists (pencillers, cleaner-uppers, eraser-monkeys, inkers, in-between-the-liners, crayonists, colorizers, mouse-clickers, and magical elves) to draw the Simpsons pretty much the same way. This process has taken us years to get right. But when I started drawing Bart, Lisa, Homer, Marge, and Maggie for the first time, there was no "right" way to draw them. I had tried, and failed, to draw like the slick professional artists I'd admired. So I gave up trying to be a drawing master and went back to doodling freakish humanoids with no chins.

For me, that was when the fun began.

Your pal,

MATT GROENING

Welcome to the world of cartooning..."Simpsons"-style! Before you roll up your sleeves and start getting your hands dirty, you'll need a few supplies. Here are some essential items, plus some fancy extras if you feel like pampering yourself.

Pencils ❶ — A standard #2 will work fine, but art pencils come in many varieties, from very soft lead (for a dark line) to very hard lead (for a light line). Pick the one that suits you best. Also, you'll notice that much of the rough sketching in this book is done with a light color pencil. Then the final line is put in with a darker lead pencil. You may want to try some of the many color pencils available and find a brand that you like.

For a sharp drawing, you'll need a sharp pencil. For that you'll need a **Pencil Sharpener ❷**. You can splurge and get a cool, noisy electric model, or economize with one of the hand-crank variety. You might also want to pick up a small portable hand-held sharpener for when you're drawing on the go.

Erasers ❸ — It's good to have a plastic eraser such as a Staedtler Mars for eradicating unwanted darker lines, and a kneaded eraser for getting rid of softer lines and removing dirt and smudges from your paper.

Speaking of **Paper ❹**, you'll need some of that, too. It'll keep you from drawing all over your walls. Any paper will do for practice, even a paper bag. But you may want a good drawing paper, layout bond or bristol board, for your more finished drawings.

Pens ❺ — In animation, the tight pencil drawings are scanned directly, but for printing purposes, a finished ink line is necessary. "Simpsons" comic books, calendars, merchandise art, etc., all require inking over the finished pencil drawings. Most "Simpsons" artists use a Rapidograph technical pen or a Micron archival ink pen to achieve those consistent "Simpsons"-style lines.

White Opaquing Paint ❻ such as Pro White is good for covering up inking mistakes, and you can easily ink back over it after it dries.

You'll rarely see a perfectly straight line in a "Simpsons" drawing, but a **T-square ❼**, **Plastic Triangle ❽**, and **Ruler ❾** will occasionally come in handy for laying out lines of perspective, floor and ceiling lines, etc., in background drawings and large props. Final lines are done without these items to give the backgrounds and props an organic hand-drawn look.

Drawing Board ❿ — A good sturdy surface is essential to a good sturdy drawing. A drawing board is ideal, but a desk or kitchen table will do as well. Some artists like to work with their paper on a flat surface, while others prefer to work at an angle. You decide what works best for you. If you can't afford an adjustable drawing board, inexpensive lightweight boards are available that you can hold on your lap or prop against the edge of a table.

If you're working at an angle, **White Paper Tape ⓫** is essential for keeping your drawing on your board and off the floor.

Lighting — Your drawing will come out better if you can actually see what you're doing. If you decide to work at a drawing board, it's a good idea to get an adjustable **Clamp-on Lamp ⓬**. Otherwise, make sure your space is well lit or that you have access to lots of **Sunlight ⓭**.

THE FAMILY

Now it can be revealed...
the jealously guarded secrets of how to draw

HOMER

Let's start with

Homer's Head

and work our way down from there.

As you can see from the rough construction lines on this drawing, Homer's skull is ball-shaped, but his overall head is sort of like a giant thumb. Once you've drawn that basic shape, you can add all the other details one by one, and Homer's head will begin to take shape, as if by magic!

But first, a few ground rules for drawing in the patented Matt Groening style.

Notice!
Big, bulgy eyeballs are a must! Shapes and sizes may vary, depending on the design of the individual character, but always keep 'em bulgy!

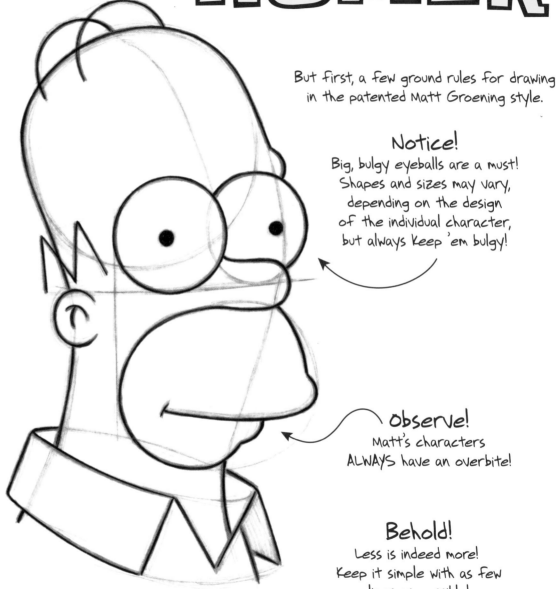

Observe!
Matt's characters ALWAYS have an overbite!

Behold!
Less is indeed more! Keep it simple with as few lines as possible!

Forehead with hair

Eyeball

Lower head

Collar

Approximately six eyeballs high!

Okay, step by step let's construct a 3/4 front view of HOMER'S HEAD.

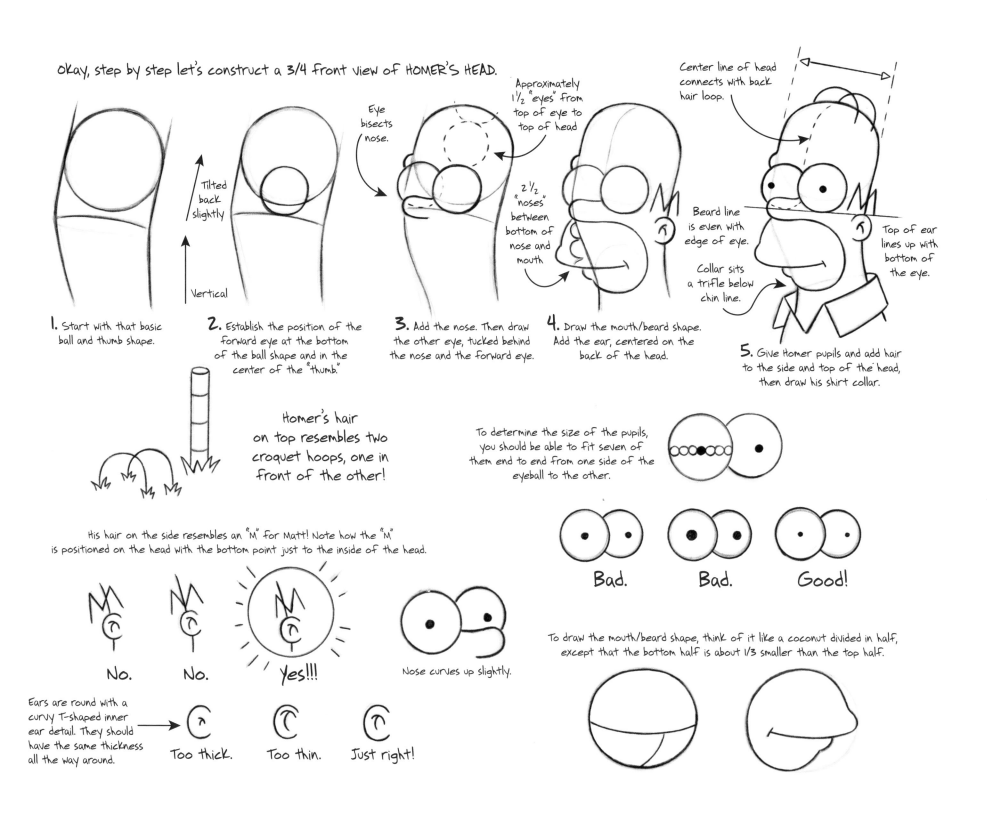

Approximately 1½ "eyes" from top of eye to top of head

Eye bisects nose.

2½ "noses" between bottom of nose and mouth

Center line of head connects with back hair loop.

Beard line is even with edge of eye.

Collar sits a trifle below chin line.

Top of ear lines up with bottom of the eye.

Tilted back slightly

Vertical

1. Start with that basic ball and thumb shape.

2. Establish the position of the forward eye at the bottom of the ball shape and in the center of the "thumb."

3. Add the nose. Then draw the other eye, tucked behind the nose and the forward eye.

4. Draw the mouth/beard shape. Add the ear, centered on the back of the head.

5. Give Homer pupils and add hair to the side and top of the head, then draw his shirt collar.

Homer's hair on top resembles two croquet hoops, one in front of the other!

To determine the size of the pupils, you should be able to fit seven of them end to end from one side of the eyeball to the other.

His hair on the side resembles an "M" for Matt! Note how the "M" is positioned on the head with the bottom point just to the inside of the head.

Bad.   Bad.   Good!

No.   No.   Yes!!!

Nose curves up slightly.

To draw the mouth/beard shape, think of it like a coconut divided in half, except that the bottom half is about 1/3 smaller than the top half.

Ears are round with a curvy T-shaped inner ear detail. They should have the same thickness all the way around.

Too thick.   Too thin.   Just right!

Now let's unlock the secrets of HOMER'S BODY

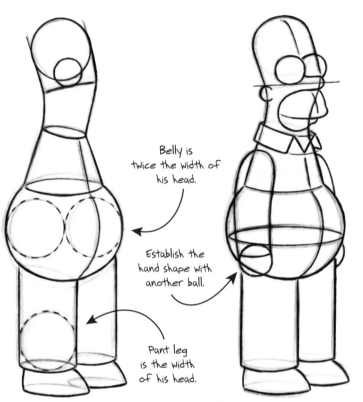

Belly is twice the width of his head.

Establish the hand shape with another ball.

Pant leg is the width of his head.

1. Block in the basic shapes.

2. Add his basic facial features, shirt collar, and arm. The front of the collar is another "M" shape.

3. Add Homer's hair and clothing details. Give him some fingers! Pants have cuffs.

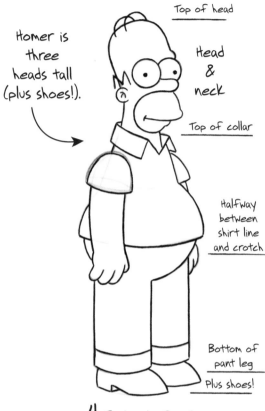

Homer is three heads tall (plus shoes!).

Top of head

Head & neck

Top of collar

Halfway between shirt line and crotch

Bottom of pant leg

Plus shoes!

4. Finish and refine the details. Shirt hangs over belly. Give the shoe a heel.

Homer's body is shaped like a giant lightbulb!

The shirtsleeve looks like a teacup.

(Oops!)

His arm is about three sleeve-lengths long!

Now it's time to put all this book learnin' into action as we examine

THE MANY MOODS OF HOMER

DEJECTED

GRUNTINGLY ANNOYED

TERRIFIED

INFURIATED

DISTRAUGHT

PEEVED

PLEASED

STUFFED

DETERMINED

AGITATED

GUILTY

STUPEFIED

TICKLED

DELIGHTED

SHOCKED

INTRIGUED

DRUNK

FEARFUL

CONDESCENDING

As you can see,
a complete range of emotions
can be achieved by changing
just a few lines.

It may sound like an oxymoron, but here's a look at

HOMER IN ACTION

Remember that Homer bends and moves like a real person (he just bends a little more!).

Notice how Homer's hair detaches from his head when in motion, to indicate speed.

His shoulders move freely up and down on his upper body, below the collar when relaxed...

...or up in front of the collar when arms are raised...

...or in motion.

Though his arm is pretty much a cylinder from shoulder to hand, it still bends at the elbow and wrist.

Wrist

Elbow

Palm is only slightly suggested.

Keep a sense of roundness to the elbow and knee joints, even when bent to the extreme.

Though static, these views of Homer from five main angles are essential to understanding how his body works, and thus being able to draw him in motion convincingly.

Front View   3/4 Front   Profile   3/4 Rear   Rear View

BODY LANGUAGE

Study these drawings and note how Homer's gestures, posture, and facial expressions all work together to tell us what he's thinking. All of these drawings are communicating something without the benefit of a voice-over or word balloon!

POINT OF VIEW

These drawings show how different perspectives affect the way we see the elements of Homer's head.

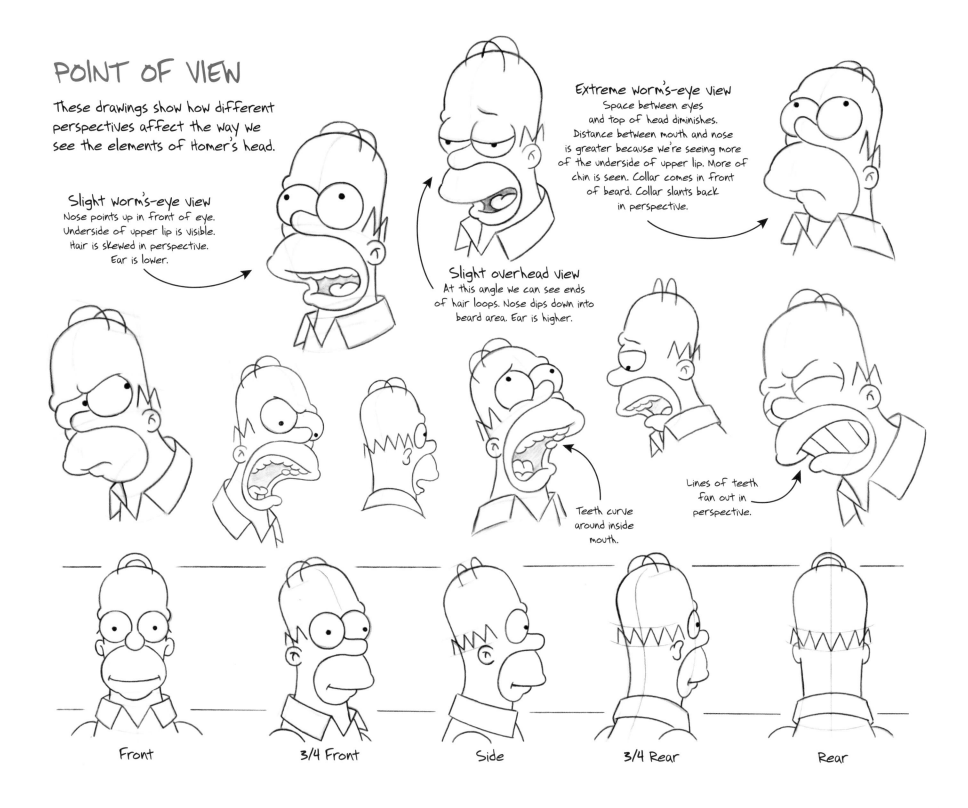

Slight worm's-eye view
Nose points up in front of eye. Underside of upper lip is visible. Hair is skewed in perspective. Ear is lower.

Extreme worm's-eye view
Space between eyes and top of head diminishes. Distance between mouth and nose is greater because we're seeing more of the underside of upper lip. More of chin is seen. Collar comes in front of beard. Collar slants back in perspective.

Slight overhead view
At this angle we can see ends of hair loops. Nose dips down into beard area. Ear is higher.

Teeth curve around inside mouth.

Lines of teeth fan out in perspective.

Front

3/4 Front

Side

3/4 Rear

Rear

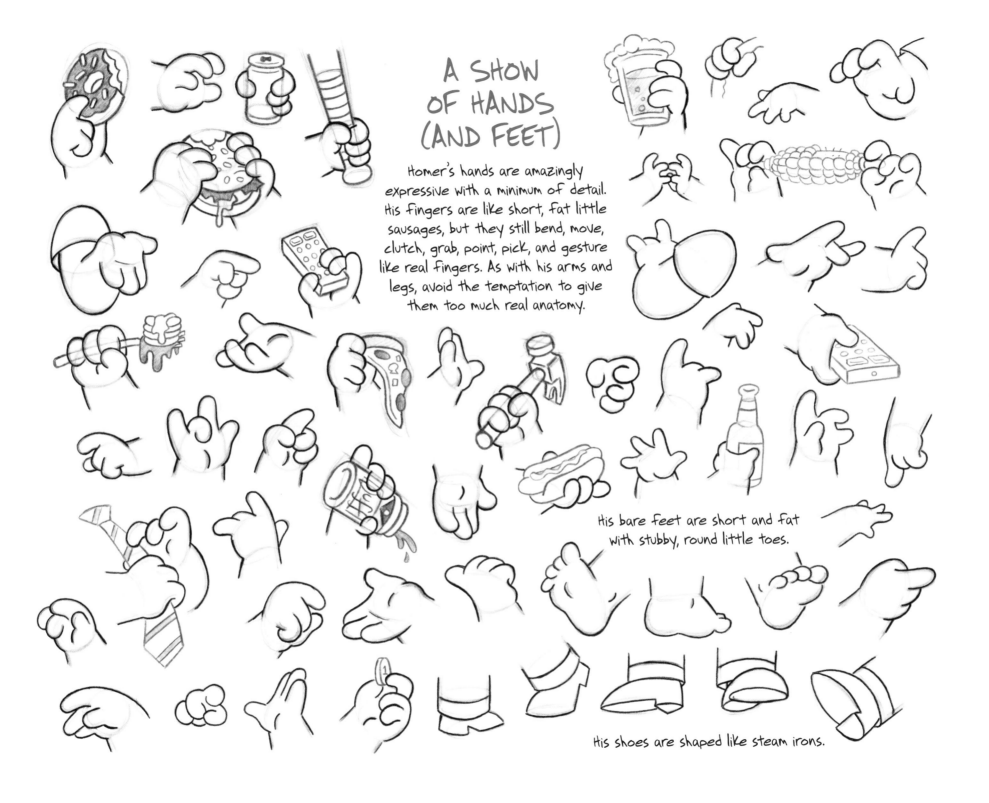

A SHOW OF HANDS (AND FEET)

Homer's hands are amazingly expressive with a minimum of detail. His fingers are like short, fat little sausages, but they still bend, move, clutch, grab, point, pick, and gesture like real fingers. As with his arms and legs, avoid the temptation to give them too much real anatomy.

His bare feet are short and fat with stubby, round little toes.

His shoes are shaped like steam irons.

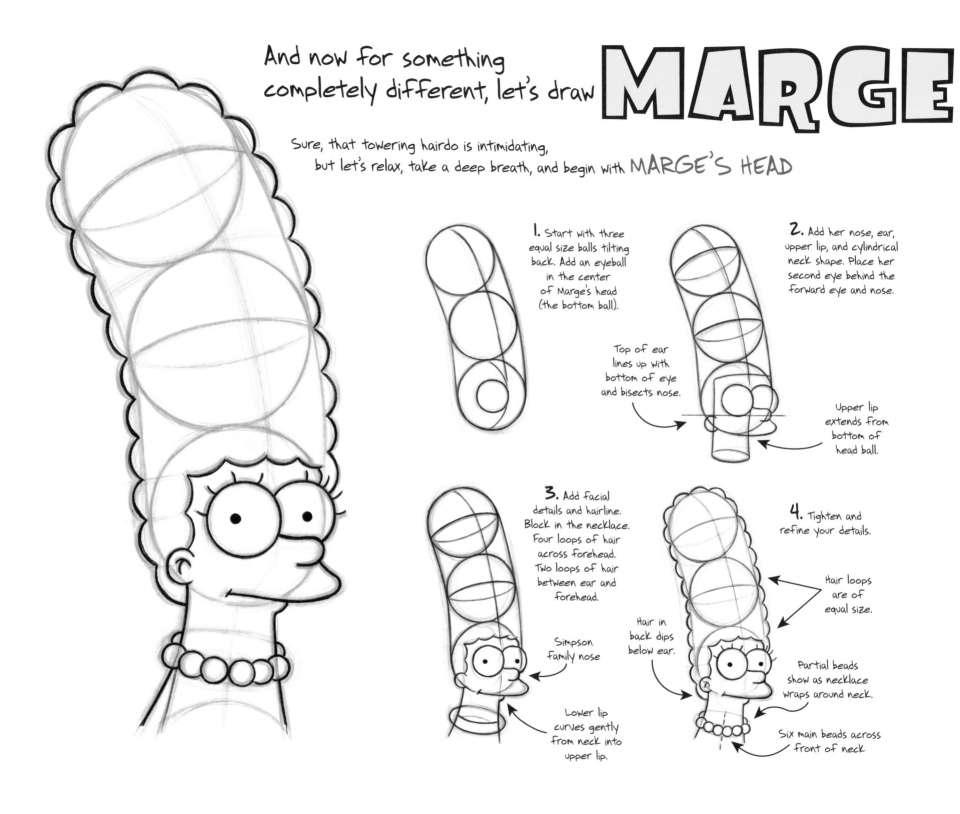

And now for something completely different, let's draw **MARGE**

Sure, that towering hairdo is intimidating,
but let's relax, take a deep breath, and begin with MARGE'S HEAD

1. Start with three equal size balls tilting back. Add an eyeball in the center of Marge's head (the bottom ball).

2. Add her nose, ear, upper lip, and cylindrical neck shape. Place her second eye behind the forward eye and nose.

Top of ear lines up with bottom of eye and bisects nose.

Upper lip extends from bottom of head ball.

3. Add facial details and hairline. Block in the necklace. Four loops of hair across forehead. Two loops of hair between ear and forehead.

Simpson family nose

Lower lip curves gently from neck into upper lip.

4. Tighten and refine your details.

Hair loops are of equal size.

Hair in back dips below ear.

Partial beads show as necklace wraps around neck.

Six main beads across front of neck

Marge's hair naturally tilts back at the top. Otherwise, it would look stiff and awkward.

There are two eyeball lengths between Marge's actual eye and the bottom of her necklace.

There is roughly one eye between the top of the nose and the mouth.

Eyelids wrap around the eyeball.

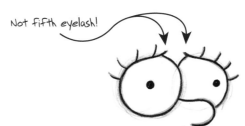

Lashes point down when eye is closed naturally.

Not fifth eyelash!

IMPORTANT!
In this tricky area, when Marge is sad or upset, make sure the overlap of the eyebrow doesn't become a fifth eyelash.

Line up hair loops to eliminate unruly hair and a huge bulge of hair at the base of the neck.

There are three pearls to each side of the center line.

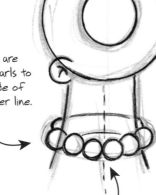

The beads touch in the center, but overlap at all other points.

The necklace is centered between the mouth and dress lines.

Give Marge's upper lip a smooth curve. Not too pointy, not too round!

For squinted eyes, lashes point up.

The expression loses energy when the lashes point down.

It's not all about the hair! Let's draw MARGE'S BODY

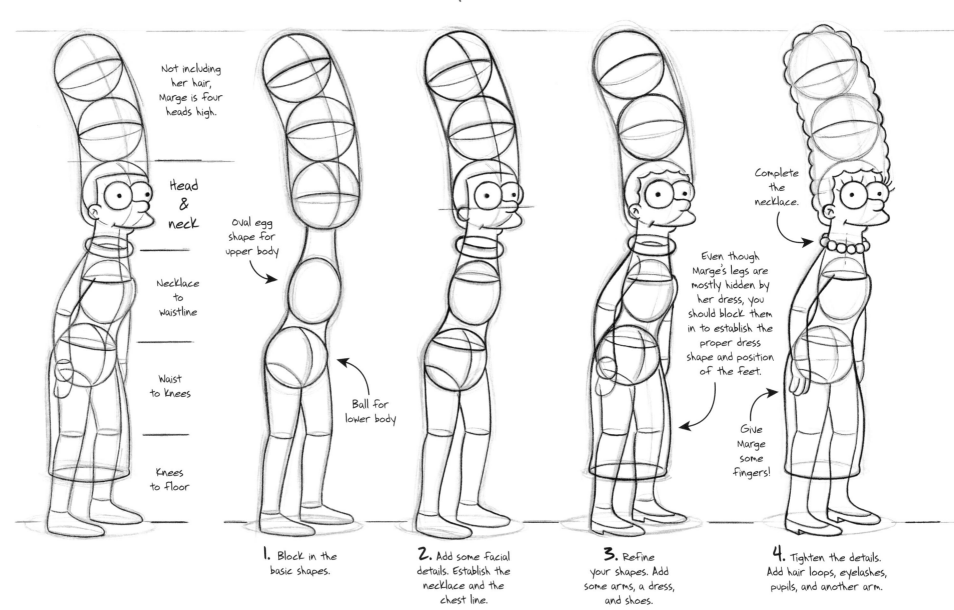

Not including her hair, Marge is four heads high.

Head & neck

Necklace to waistline

Waist to knees

Knees to floor

Oval egg shape for upper body

Ball for lower body

Complete the necklace.

Even though Marge's legs are mostly hidden by her dress, you should block them in to establish the proper dress shape and position of the feet.

Give Marge some fingers!

1. Block in the basic shapes.

2. Add some facial details. Establish the necklace and the chest line.

3. Refine your shapes. Add some arms, a dress, and shoes.

4. Tighten the details. Add hair loops, eyelashes, pupils, and another arm.

Believe it or not, Marge has a consistent number of hair loops.

3

3

3

There are eleven loops on the front side of her head.

There are twelve loops on the backside of her head.

There are four loops of hair across forehead...

...and two loops of hair between ear and forehead.

Marge's eyelashes radiate out from a vanishing point at the center of the eye and are evenly spaced.

As with all Simpson family members, Marge's nose curves up just a bit.

The eyelashes curve out slightly and are of equal length.

YES!

NO!

The shoulder line flows gracefully into the neck.

1/3

1/3

1/3

When arm is in a relaxed position at Marge's side, her knuckles are even with her crotch line.

The dress line should be placed 2/3 of the way up the oval chest shape.

Shoe is flush with ankle.

Show dimension on heel of shoe.

Show thickness of dress fabric.

Dress hangs over her legs.

Soft bump for lower lip.

Now let's look at THE MYRIAD MOODS OF MARGE

EMBARRASSED   CURIOUS   INFURIATED   WORRIED

MAD   EXCITED   HAPPY   EXHAUSTED   PEEVED

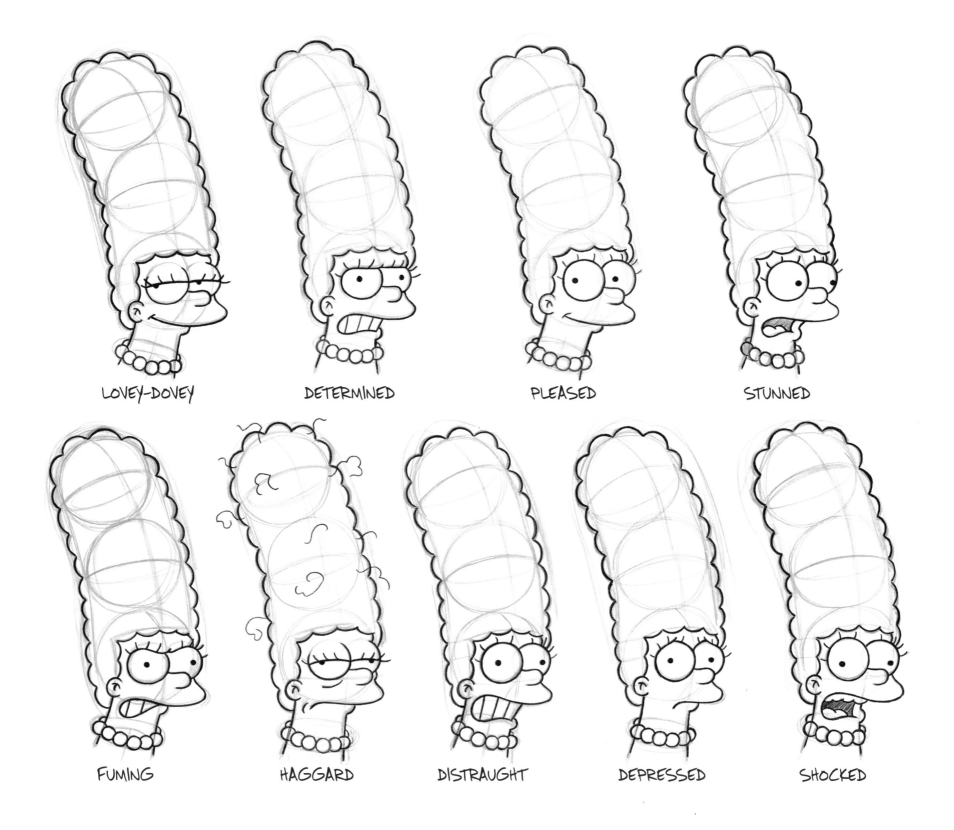

LOVEY-DOVEY   DETERMINED   PLEASED   STUNNED

FUMING   HAGGARD   DISTRAUGHT   DEPRESSED   SHOCKED

Stay out of her way! It's MARGE ON THE MOVE

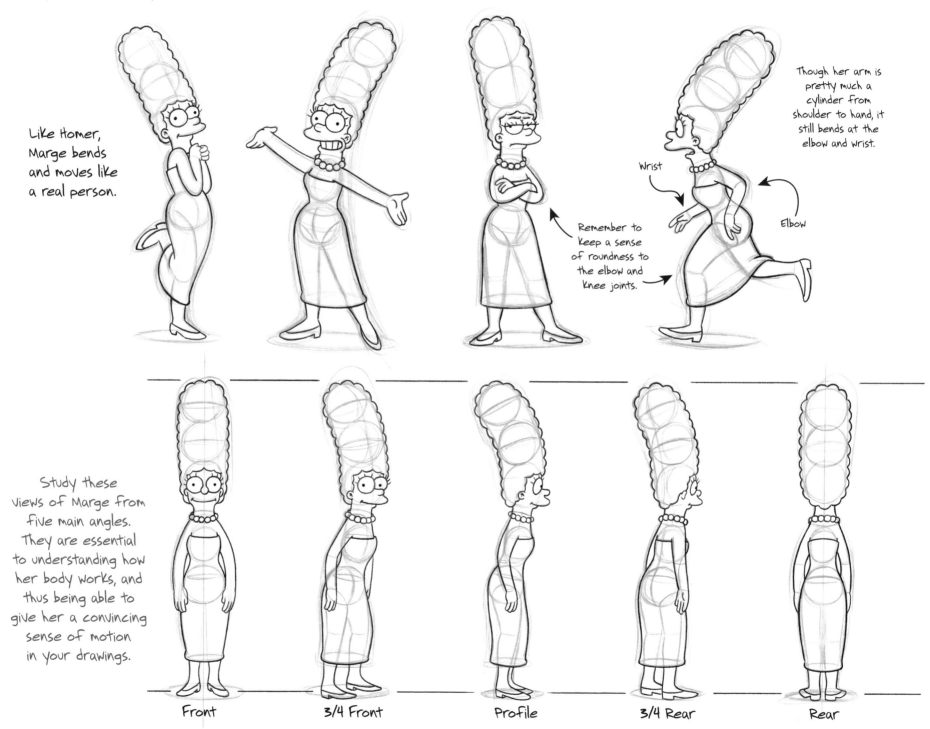

Like Homer, Marge bends and moves like a real person.

Remember to keep a sense of roundness to the elbow and knee joints.

Though her arm is pretty much a cylinder from shoulder to hand, it still bends at the elbow and wrist.

Wrist

Elbow

Study these views of Marge from five main angles. They are essential to understanding how her body works, and thus being able to give her a convincing sense of motion in your drawings.

Front

3/4 Front

Profile

3/4 Rear

Rear

SELECTIVE PERSPECTIVE

These drawings show how different points of view affect how we see the elements of Marge's head.

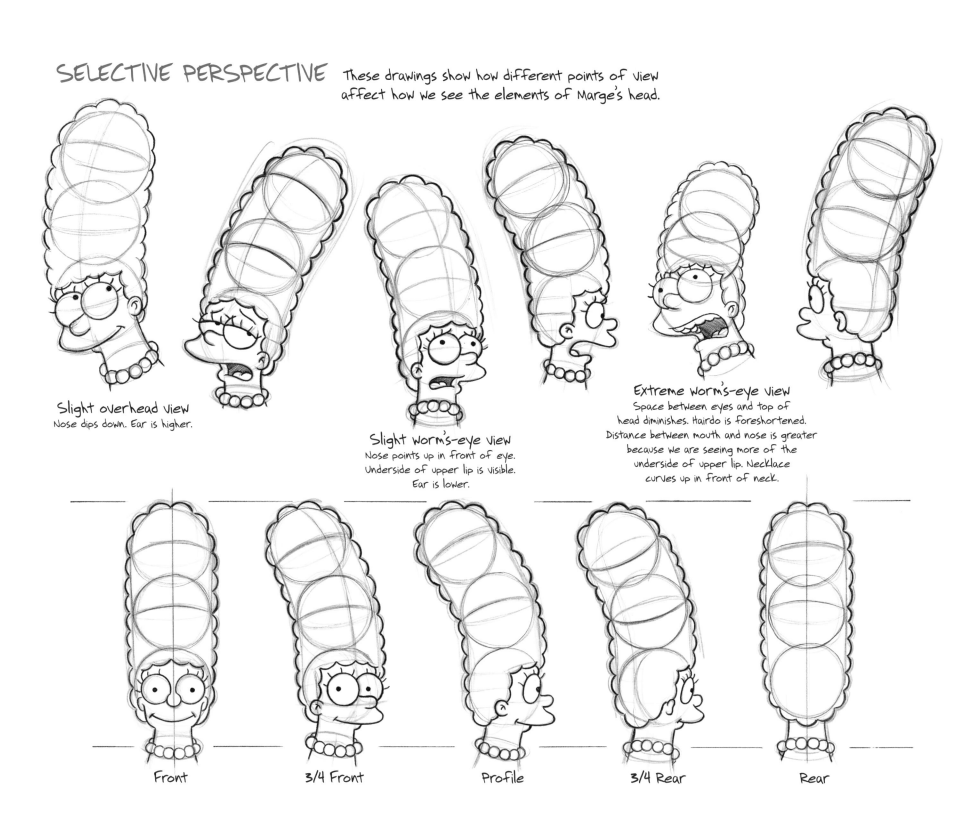

Slight overhead view
Nose dips down. Ear is higher.

Slight worm's-eye view
Nose points up in front of eye.
Underside of upper lip is visible.
Ear is lower.

Extreme worm's-eye view
Space between eyes and top of
head diminishes. Hairdo is foreshortened.
Distance between mouth and nose is greater
because we are seeing more of the
underside of upper lip. Necklace
curves up in front of neck.

Front   3/4 Front   Profile   3/4 Rear   Rear

A HANDY-DANDY GUIDE TO MARGE'S HANDS (AND FEET)

Whereas Homer's fingers are short and stubby, Marge's are long and slender. Because of this, there may be more temptation to give them too much real anatomy. Don't give in! You can keep them simple, yet still expressive.

Like her hands, Marge's feet are fairly long and slender. Her shoes fit snugly.

You'll amaze your friends and confound your enemies when you unlock the mysteries of how to draw

First, let's start at the command center, BART'S HEAD

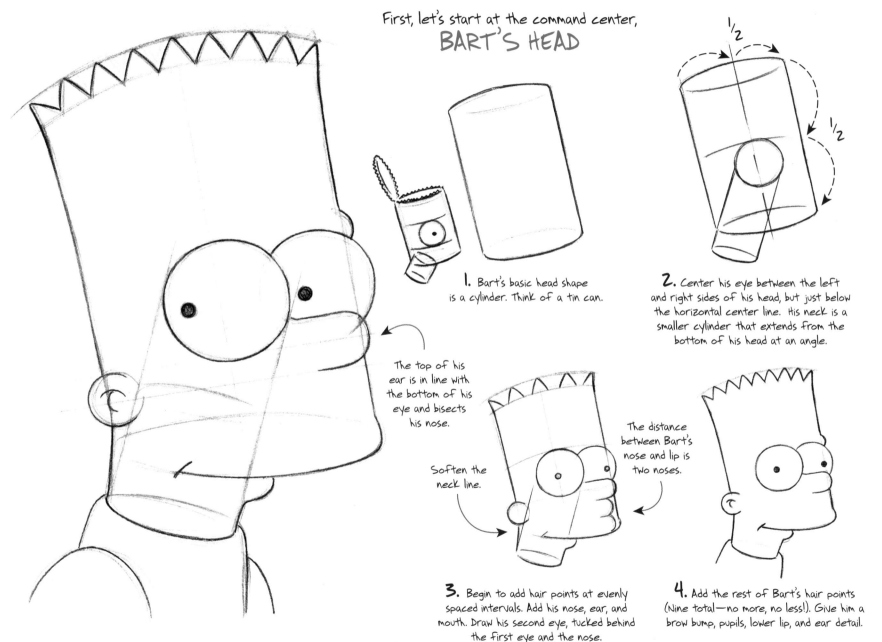

1. Bart's basic head shape is a cylinder. Think of a tin can.

2. Center his eye between the left and right sides of his head, but just below the horizontal center line. His neck is a smaller cylinder that extends from the bottom of his head at an angle.

The top of his ear is in line with the bottom of his eye and bisects his nose.

The distance between Bart's nose and lip is two noses.

Soften the neck line.

3. Begin to add hair points at evenly spaced intervals. Add his nose, ear, and mouth. Draw his second eye, tucked behind the first eye and the nose.

4. Add the rest of Bart's hair points (Nine total—no more, no less!). Give him a brow bump, pupils, lower lip, and ear detail.

The top of each hair point is rounded and each point bows out slightly.

TOO PUFFY!

TOO SHARP!

A-OH-KAY!

Bart's head is roughly 4 ½ eyes high.

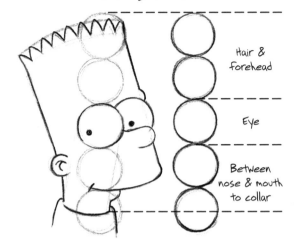

Hair & forehead

Eye

Between nose & mouth to collar

Like all the Simpsons characters, Bart's teeth are in a conical arrangement. Whether the mouth is open or closed, they should retain this shape.

The teeth follow the direction of the neck line.

Bart's eyeball is approximately seven pupils wide...

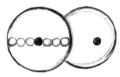

...like so!

As with all Simpsons family members, Bart's nose curves up just a bit.

When drawing the classic Bart grin, make sure you have at least three interior tooth lines.

Note also how the spacing decreases as the teeth curve away at the front.

There is a very slight flare on the sides of Bart's hair.

His neck inserts into the shirt collar.

Now, unless you want to draw only close-ups, we'd better learn how to draw

BART'S BODY

Bart is two heads tall (plus shoes!).

Tin can head

Thimble chest

Ball-shaped belly

Steam iron feet

Tubular legs

1. Start by blocking in the basic shapes.

2. Add eyes and arms. Establish a center line for reference when adding details.

3. Add nose, ear, and fingers. Define Bart's hair and clothing.

4. Put in pupils, ear detail, and shoe detail.

Top of head to shirt collar

Shirt collar to top of socks

Plus shoes!

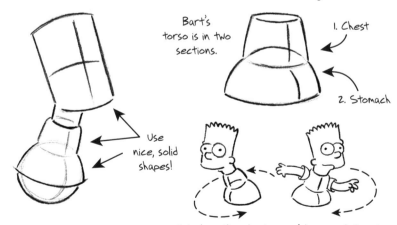

Use nice, solid shapes!

Bart's torso is in two sections.

1. Chest

2. Stomach

Note how the chest can slide around the stomach.

Bart's T-shirt has a thickness to it. Make sure it wraps around the form of the neck.

In a normal standing pose, Bart's legs and feet should be firmly planted on the ground and evenly spaced, supporting the rest of his body.

Hair points are slightly rounded.

YES!

...not sharp!

NO!

Chest and back lines bow out slightly.

Bart's shirtsleeve is a wee bit tapered at the top, like the tip of a bullet...

...as opposed to Homer's, which is more round, like a teacup.

Hair flares out a little

Straight

Graceful curve to neck

Fingers are short and fat (a Simpsons family trait!).

Don't forget to add the sole!

Shirt hangs over pants.

Socks are donut-shaped.

The circle detail on Bart's shoes is on the inside only!

So is the upper lip...

YES!

NO!

Eyebrow bump is smooth and graceful.

...and the lower lip!

YES!

NO!

As with all Simpsons family members, the nose curves up slightly where it meets the eye.

Bart doesn't have a full belly like Homer (not yet, anyway!). The line defining his stomach has a break in it.

THE MULTITUDINOUS MOODS OF BART

Once again, notice how with minor variations in the mouth and eyes, you can create a wide range of emotions!

BORED

STUNNED

HUNGRY

ANGRY

HYSTERICAL

CONFIDENT

DISTRESSED

UNSURE

ANGST-RIDDEN

WOOZY

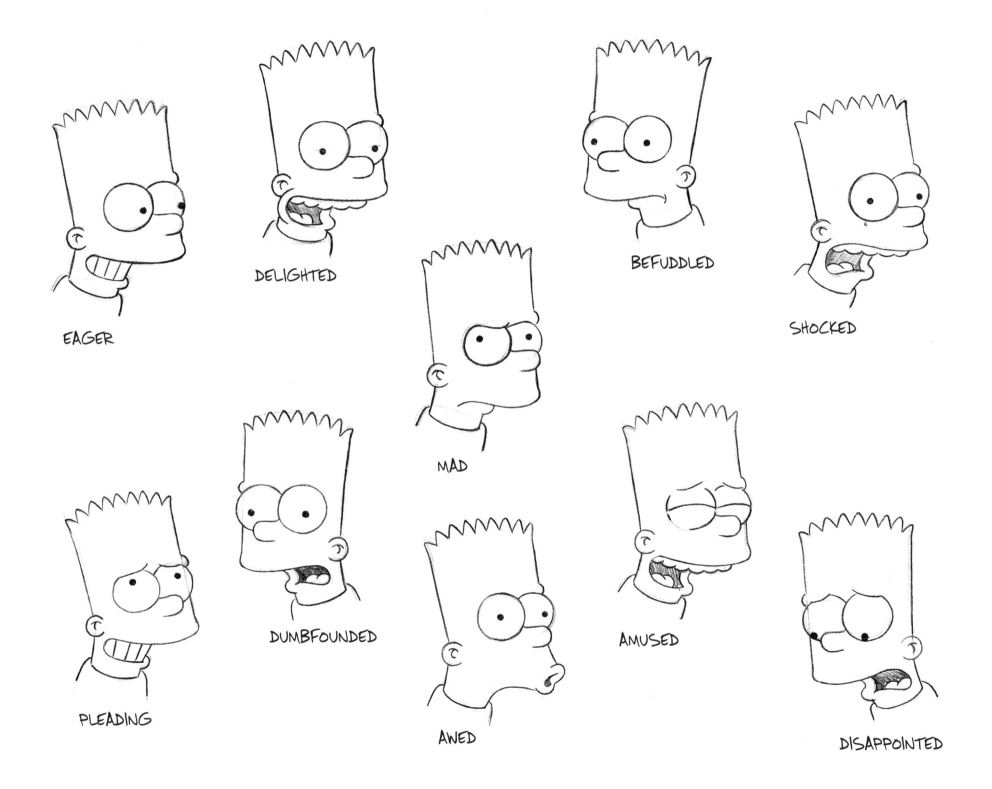

EAGER

DELIGHTED

BEFUDDLED

SHOCKED

MAD

PLEADING

DUMBFOUNDED

AWED

AMUSED

DISAPPOINTED

He may be known as an underachiever, but that doesn't mean
Bart just stands around. You need to learn how to draw BART IN ACTION

Think of the figure moving in three-dimensional space, not on a flat two-dimensional surface.

Notice how Bart's shoulders are mobile. They can swing around.

It's important to establish the line of action in any pose, then build your drawing along that line.

Inside of shirtsleeve visible

Arm coming forward in space

Palm back

Arm going back in space

Palm out

Underside of shoe

Foot coming forward in space

Foot going back in space

As Bart leans forward in this pose, notice how the weight of his body is on one foot.

Hair moves to indicate speed

Knees bent, showing weight of body on legs

Note how shirt flies up to indicate the up and down movement of Bart's body as he runs.

Even though Bart is leaning forward, he's solidly planted on the ground.

Foot planted directly beneath head for great balance

The index finger extends directly from the line of the arm.

Though his arm is pretty much a cylinder from shoulder to hand, it still bends at the elbow and wrist.

Elbow

Wrist

Palm is only slightly suggested.

Keep a sense of roundness to the elbow and knee joints, even when bent to the extreme.

Though static, these views of Bart from five main angles are essential to understanding how his body works, and thus being able to draw him in motion convincingly.

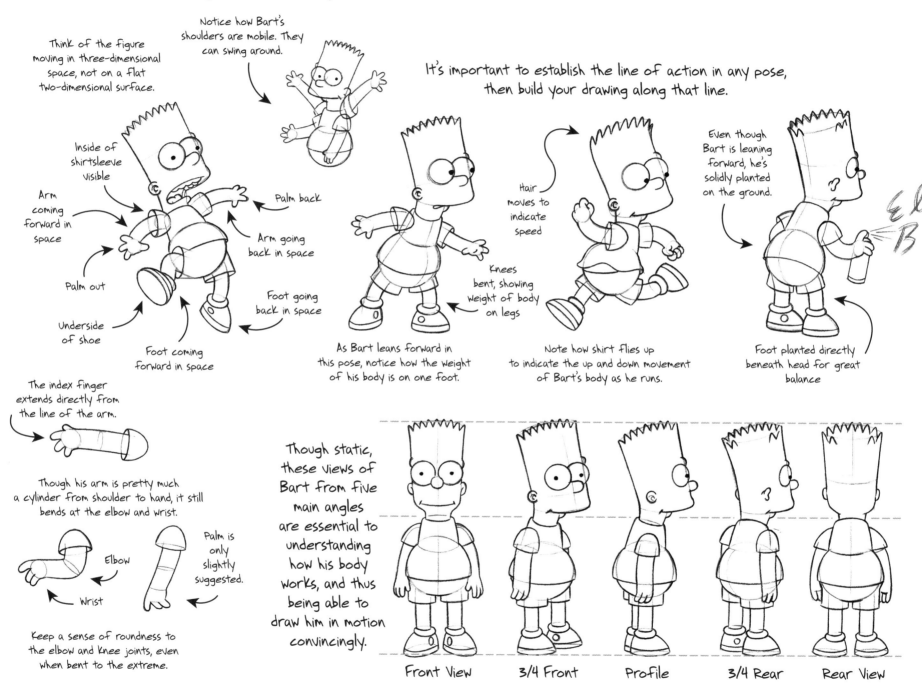

Front View   3/4 Front   Profile   3/4 Rear   Rear View

BODIES OF EVIDENCE

Study these drawings and notice how the expressions,
gestures, and motion combine to tell the story.

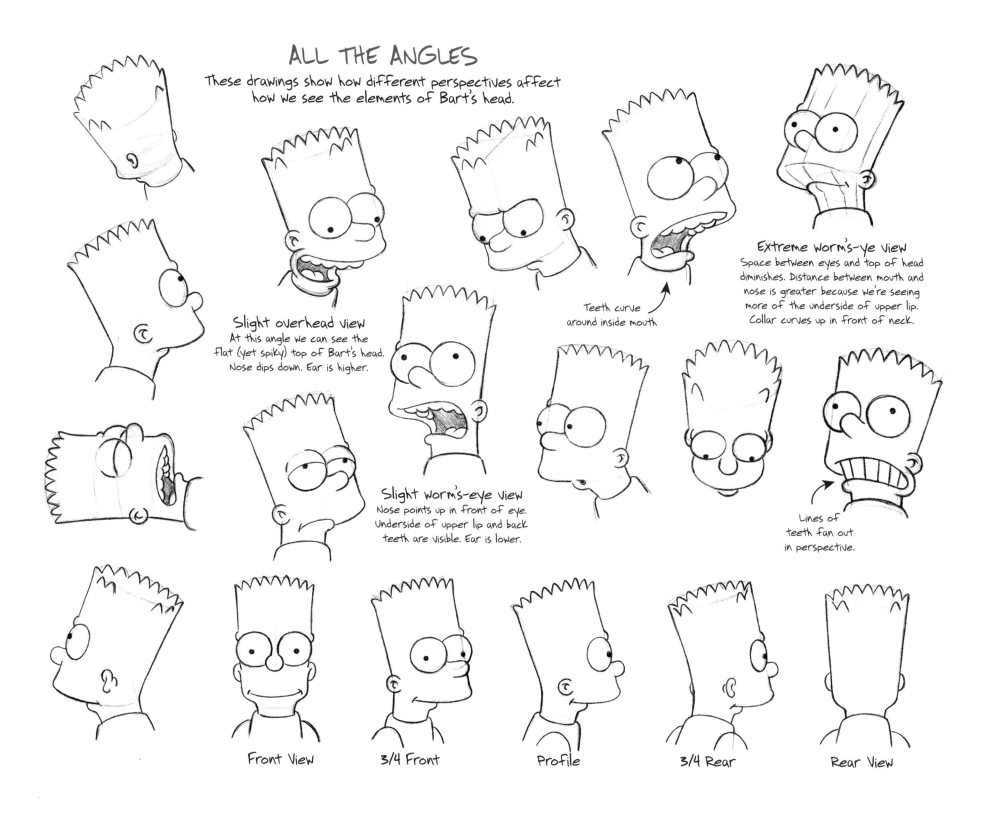

ALL THE ANGLES

These drawings show how different perspectives affect how we see the elements of Bart's head.

Slight overhead view
At this angle we can see the flat (yet spiky) top of Bart's head. Nose dips down. Ear is higher.

Slight worm's-eye view
Nose points up in front of eye. Underside of upper lip and back teeth are visible. Ear is lower.

Teeth curve around inside mouth

Extreme worm's-ye view
Space between eyes and top of head diminishes. Distance between mouth and nose is greater because we're seeing more of the underside of upper lip. Collar curves up in front of neck.

Lines of teeth fan out in perspective.

Front View   3/4 Front   Profile   3/4 Rear   Rear View

HAND JIVE
(AND FOOT FRIVOLITY)

Like his father, Bart's hands are amazingly expressive with a minimum of detail. Also like Homer, his fingers resemble short, fat little sausages, but they still bend, move, clutch, swipe, point, flick, and rudely gesture like real fingers.

His shoes are shaped like steam irons.

His bare feet are short and fat with stubby, round little toes.

In an overachieving mood? Okay then! Let's draw **LISA**

We'll get right to the point...

...(actually eight points) with LISA'S HEAD!

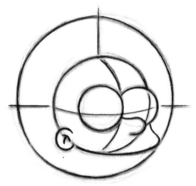

Head circle

Eye

1. Start with two concentric circles. These will become Lisa's head and eye.

2. Add the ear, nose, and upper lip, then draw the other eye behind the forward eye and the nose. Now add the hair circle. The hair circle is not concentric with the head and eye.

Upper lip is not too pointy, not too round!

3. Block in Lisa's hair, neck, and necklace. Establish horizontal and vertical center lines on the head. Divide hair points into three groups based on these center lines.

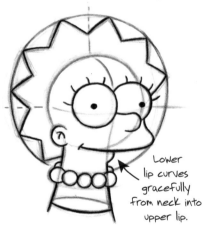

Lower lip curves gracefully from neck into upper lip.

4. Tighten up and add details: pupils, eyelashes, necklace.

3 **3**

2

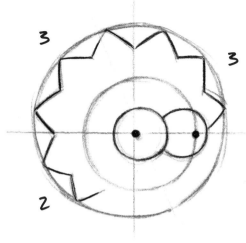

Lisa has eight points of hair, which are divided into groups of three and three (above the horizontal center) and two (below the horizon).

The points of Lisa's hair are soft, arching triangles with lightly rounded tips.

No.

YES!

Arc → ← Arc

Rounded meeting point

Eyelashes
Not too short. Not too long.

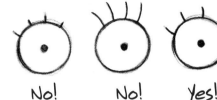

No!   No!   Yes!

Even space between lashes.

Like Marge, Lisa's lashes curve out from a vanishing point in the center of the eye.

Lisa has four lashes on each eye.

Some notes about teeth!

Lisa generally has five teeth showing when mouth is open.

When drawing a toothy grin, always slant the forward tooth in line with the neck.

As with other Simpsons family members, Lisa's teeth are in a conical arrangement. Whether the mouth is open or closed, they should retain this shape.

Teeth are never drawn in double rows like this—EVER!

Some fresh notes on the eyes
These apply to ALL Simpsons characters!

Never cross the eyes!   No!

No!

When eyes are closed or half open, don't use a complete circle for the eyelid.

Yeah!

1 ¾ eyes from top of eyes to top of hair

Eye

1 ½ eyes to bottom of necklace

Lisa's head is 4¼ eyeballs tall.

Think of Lisa's necklace as a donut around her neck. Draw through her neck to see the whole shape.

Necklace has five beads in front, with two partially showing in back on either side.

Good!

Never!

occasionally, you may want to draw Lisa from a slightly more frontal view. When doing this, leave a space between her eyes. This goes for the entire Simpsons family too.

From this slightly more frontal view, Lisa has an extra hair point showing.

Add hair point here!

Now that you've mastered the mathematics of her head, let's sum it all up with LISA'S BODY

1. By now you know that you block in the basic shapes first.

Head ball is bigger than belly ball.

Cylindrical legs

Steam iron shoes

2. Add head details as previously directed. Establish the necklace, dress shape, and shoes.

Space from top of necklace to mouth is equal to space between bottom of necklace and top of dress.

3. Add arms and dress detail. Continue to add facial elements. seven dress points, evenly spaced.

4. Refine the shapes and add final details. Put in beads of necklace. Add fingers. Complete shoe detail.

Lisa is two heads tall (plus shoes!).

Like Marge, her shoulder flows gracefully into her neck.

Whether we're seeing her arm or her back, they both sweep up nicely into her neck.

Note the hidden lines.

IMPORTANT!
In rough drawings, always draw through forward elements like arms and legs to establish the form underneath.

No!

Avoid bulging shoulders.

Oh, but yes!

Note how cylindrical legs insert into ball of lower body.

As with all Simpsons Family members, the nose curves up slightly where it meets the eye.

The Simpsons family trait continues: fingers are short and fat.

Her ear straddles the main head ball shape.

On Lisa, the neck line connects with the ear.

Like her hair, Lisa's dress points bow out slightly and are lightly rounded at the tips.

Graceful curve to the neck

Chest and back lines curve in slightly.

Use nice, swooping arcs for the straps on Lisa's shoes.

THE MANIFOLD
MOODS OF LISA

DISAPPOINTED

EMBARRASSED

TERRIFIED

HAPPY

SPECULATIVE

CROSS

AWED

ANNOYED

PLEASED

DISTRESSED

PEEVISH

MIRTHFUL

ASTONISHED

BLUE

SARCASTIC

PLAYFUL

APPALLED

DREAMY

GIGGLY

MELANCHOLY

She doesn't just talk the talk, Lisa walks the walk (and runs, and jumps, and skips...). Let's learn how to draw LISA IN ACTION

All of the previous notes regarding movement apply to Lisa too, but notice the graceful, flowing lines in these Lisa action poses.

Note the line of action in this running pose.

Hair moves to indicate speed.

Note how her dress flies up and back to further indicate her body's forward motion.

As Lisa leans forward in this pose, notice how the weight of her body is on this foot.

Notice how this leg is placed directly under her head for good balance as she leans forward.

Knees are bent, showing weight of body on legs.

Study these stationary views of Lisa from five angles to understand how her body works. This will allow you to draw her in motion more convincingly.

Front View

3/4 Front

Profile

3/4 Rear

Rear View

FRESH PERSPECTIVES

These diverse views illustrate how different perspectives affect the way we see the elements of Lisa's head.

Slight overhead view
At this angle there is more space between Lisa's eyes and the top of her head. Nose dips down. Ear is higher. Lower lip and neck are diminished.

Slight worm's-eye view
Nose points up in front of eye. Underside of upper lip is visible. Ear is lower.

Extreme worm's-eye view
Space between eyes and top of head diminishes. Distance between mouth and nose is greater because we're seeing more of the underside of upper lip. Necklace curves up in front of neck.

Front

3/4 Front

Profile

3/4 Rear

Rear

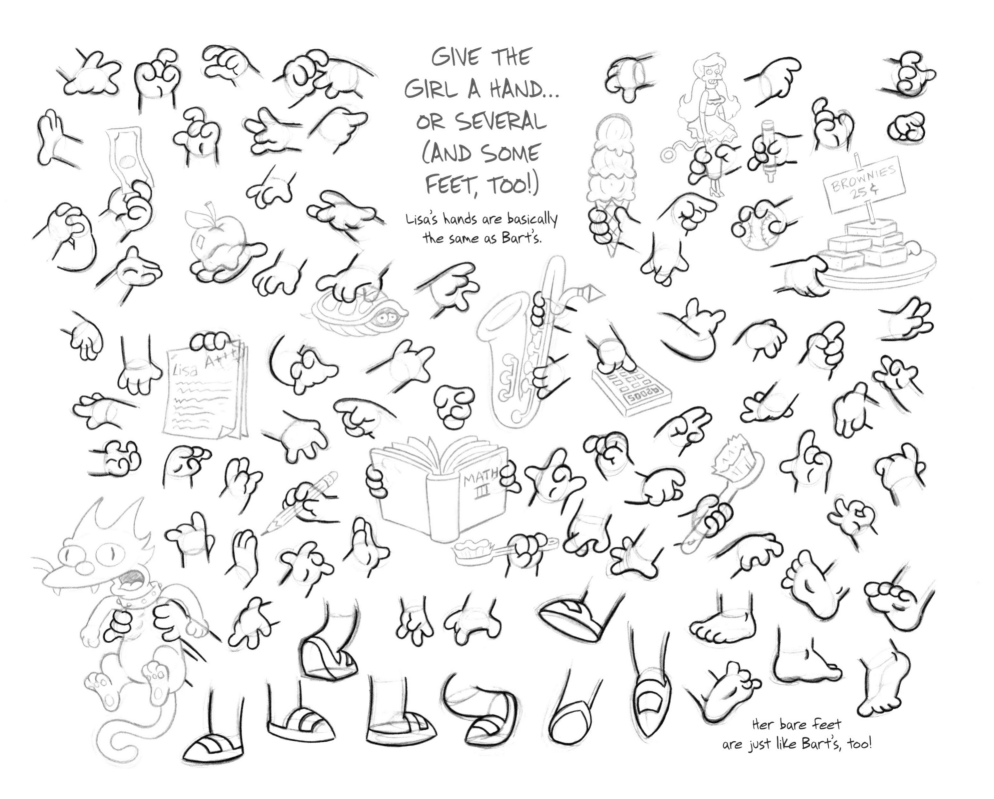

GIVE THE
GIRL A HAND...
OR SEVERAL
(AND SOME
FEET, TOO!)

Lisa's hands are basically
the same as Bart's.

Her bare feet
are just like Bart's, too!

Now that you have Lisa down pat, it'll be a snap to draw

MAGGIE

As you would expect by now, we'll start with
MAGGIE'S HEAD

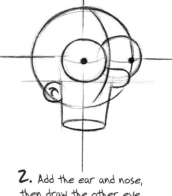

Head circle

Eye

I. Start with a donut.
(No sprinkles, please!)

2. Add the ear and nose,
then draw the other eye
behind the forward eye and
the nose. Add the cylindrical
neck shape.

3. Block in her pacifier and add
the hair circle. The hair circle is not
concentric with the head and eye. Block
in Maggie's hair. You can also draw an inside
circle to define how deep each hair point
should go. Maggie has 8 points of hair, but
they are not in the same arrangement
as Lisa's. See if you can spot
the difference!

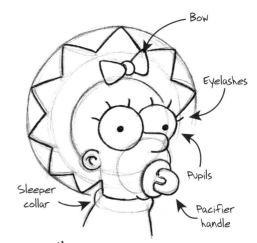

Bow

Eyelashes

Pupils

Sleeper
collar

Pacifier
handle

4. Add details and tighten.

MAGGIE'S PACIFIER SUCKING CYCLE

Maggie's eyelashes are like Lisa's, except that she only has three of them! They are of equal length and are equally spaced.

No!   Yes!

Maggie's head is 4 1/2 eyeballs high.

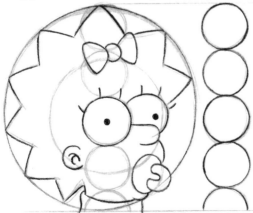

The points of Maggie's hair are soft, arching triangles with lightly rounded tips.

Incorrect!

Correct!

Correct-a-mundo!

Right!   Wrong! (Too pointy!)

3   3

3

2

Hair points are arranged in a 3-3-2 setup on a tilted axis.

If you think you can get away with just drawing a formless sleeper under Maggie's head, think again!

There's a tiny baby figure under that thing. So let's learn how to draw...

MAGGIE'S BODY

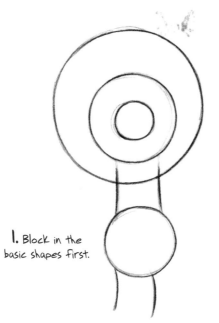

1. Block in the basic shapes first.

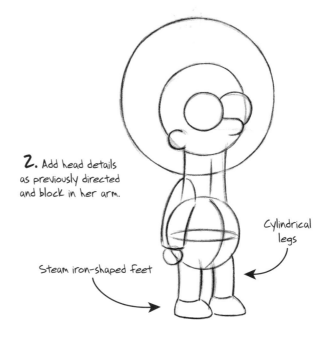

2. Add head details as previously directed and block in her arm.

Cylindrical legs

Steam iron-shaped feet

3. Continue to add facial elements.

4. Refine the shapes and add final details. Don't forget the tiny fingers!

5. Now that you've established Maggie's body, you can add her sleeper. Wrap it snugly around her upper body and let it hang loosely from her belly. Knee and foot are slightly suggested.

Maggie is only two heads tall.

Maggie's belly ball is 3/4 the size of her head ball.

Head ball

Belly ball

From the tip of her highest hair point to her collar

Unlike Lisa, Maggie's neck line does not connect with her ear.

Remember to keep her hands tiny and her fingers short and fat.

From her collar to the floor

Use smooth, rounded lines for the fabric of her sleeper. Fabric should have a weight and thickness like real baby clothes.

Maggie's body normally stays hidden inside her sleeper. Body shapes are revealed when necessary to describe her form.

The shapes that make up Maggie's body remain the same, no matter what view she is seen from.

Front

3/4 Front

Profile

3/4 Rear

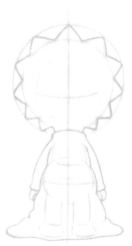

7/8 Rear

Rear

Think a baby can't communicate as well as her parents
or older siblings? Well, think again! Here are

THE MANY MOODS OF MAGGIE

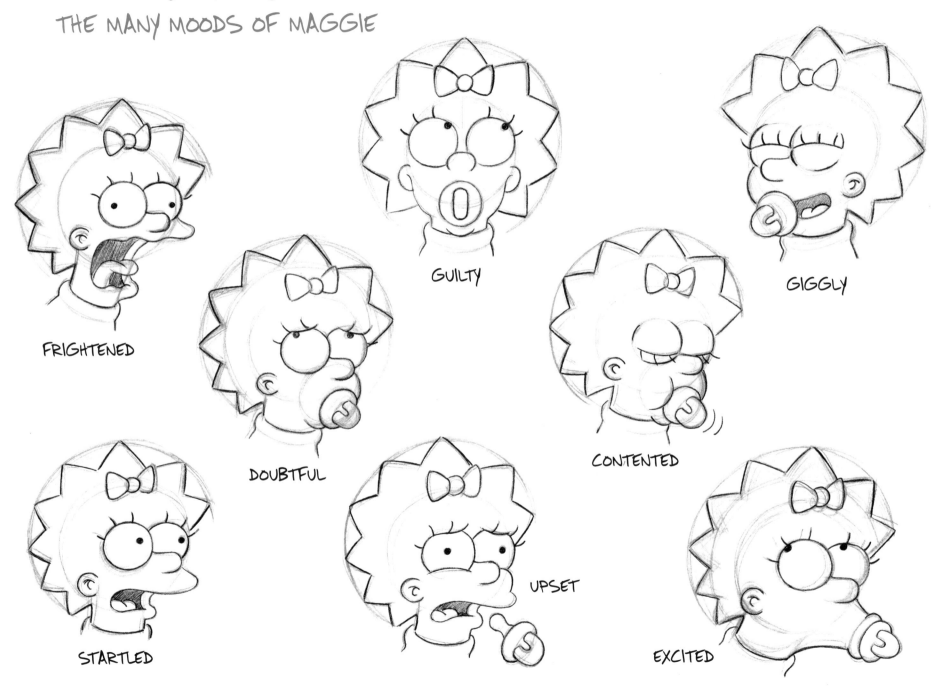

FRIGHTENED

DOUBTFUL

GUILTY

GIGGLY

CONTENTED

STARTLED

UPSET

EXCITED

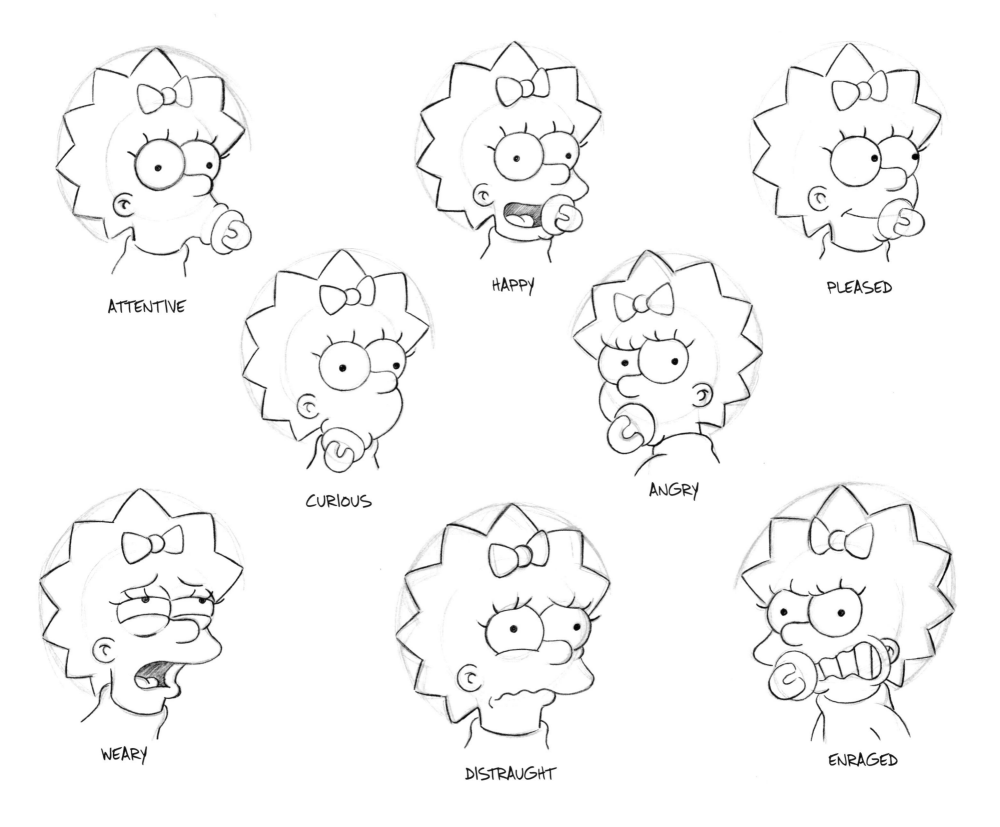

ATTENTIVE

HAPPY

PLEASED

CURIOUS

ANGRY

WEARY

DISTRAUGHT

ENRAGED

Ask any mother, babies can be a handful, and the Simpsons'
baby is no exception. You'll want to learn to draw

MAGGIE IN MOTION

In action shots
reveal parts
of Maggie under
her sleeper, like a
knee or a foot.

B

K

Try to capture
a sense of the
awkward motion
of a real baby.

Gestures
should be cute
and babylike.

POINT OF VIEW

As with Lisa, note how different perspectives affect how we see the elements of Maggie's head.

Slight worm's-eye view
Nose points up in front of eye.
Bow is higher on head.

Slight overhead view
At this angle there is more space between Maggie's eyes and the top of her head. Bow does not break hairline as usual. Nose dips down toward pacifier. Ear is higher.

Extreme worm's-eye view
Space between eyes and top of head diminishes. Distance between pacifier and nose is greater. Collar curves up in front of neck.

HANDS (AND FEET) ACROSS THE NURSERY

Maggie's hands are basically the same as Lisa's, but much smaller. Even though they're small with stubby little fingers, Maggie's hands can bend, move, clutch, grab, point, pick, and gesture like any other character's.

THE SUPPORTING CAST

Let's leave the primary Simpson family members for a while and explore some of the secondary characters, starting with

GRAMPA

By now you should be pretty familiar with the method of building a character from familiar shapes, so we'll dispense with the usual construction notes and just focus on specific details that make the residents of Springfield unique!

1. Use cone shapes for Grampa's head.

2. This cone establishes his hair.

3. Four points of hair, similar in shape to Bart's

Three folds of skin

Wrinkled upper lip

4. Old-age bumps and wrinkles

Grampa's eyes are usually at half-mast.

1.

Hunched posture

Belly line flows smoothly into chest.

2.

3.

Slippers

4.

Wavy lines give Grampa's clothing a wrinkled look.

INSIDE TIP!
Grampa wears dentures! If you ever draw him without them, don't forget that they are what keep his lips from receding into his mouth!

The Many Moods of Grampa

BARNEY

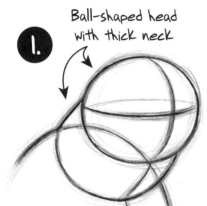

Ball-shaped head with thick neck

1.

2.

Space between baggy eyes

Ear set high on head, even with eyes.

3.

Despite his good nature, Barney often has a furrowed brow.

4.

Nose curves up.

5.

Three teeth show when mouth is closed.

Hair is sharp and bushy.

6.

1 2 3 4 5

1.

Belly is a large oval.

Barney is five heads tall.

2.

Posture is slouched.

Legs are set wide apart.

Arms are fat at the shoulder and taper down to thinner wrists.

3.

Completed head is thrust forward, even with belly.

4.

V-neck shirt exposes chest hair.

Too tight shirt exposes belly.

Stripes on shoes

INSIDE TIP!

Barney's hair does have a specific design consisting of thirteen points!

Two-pronged cowlick

Four points on top with a part in the center

Three bushy points in back

Two points on forehead

One short point and one long point for sideburns

The Many Moods of Barney

MILHOUSE

1. Milhouse has a cylindrical head with convex sides. The top of his head and his mouth line are convergent.

Eyes are centered vertically on head and set very wide apart.

Neck is short and conical.

2. Nose is big and round and takes up 3/4 of the space between the center of his head and his mouth.

Glasses have thick lenses.

3. Add hair in two pieces.

Ear sits slightly above the bottom line of his eyes.

4. Add stem and bridge to glasses.

The stem rests against his head above his ear. Milhouse has thick, rectangular eyebrows.

1.

Milhouse has a body similar to Bart's, but with a wider, shorter chest.

Feet are small and wedge-shaped.

2.

Arms are much wider than legs.

His legs are long and thin and set wide apart.

3.

T-shirt rides high on belly.

Shorts are wide and long.

4.

Sleeves are cup-shaped.

INSIDE TIP!
When Milhouse takes off his glasses, his eyes are two little dots. When he closes his eyes, they are two little lines.

THE MANY MOODS OF MILHOUSE

MRS. KRABAPPEL

1. Edna Krabappel's head is a ball-shape centered on a conical neck.

2. Eyes are oval and set apart.

Rounded nose points down toward upper lip.

Ear is set well below the eyes.

3. Draw three circular shapes to establish her hairdo.

Don't forget the earring!

4. Three lines indicate back sweep of hair.

Mrs. K has four short eyelashes per eye.

Add texture to hair.

She's Bart's teacher, so remember to add tired bags under her eyes!

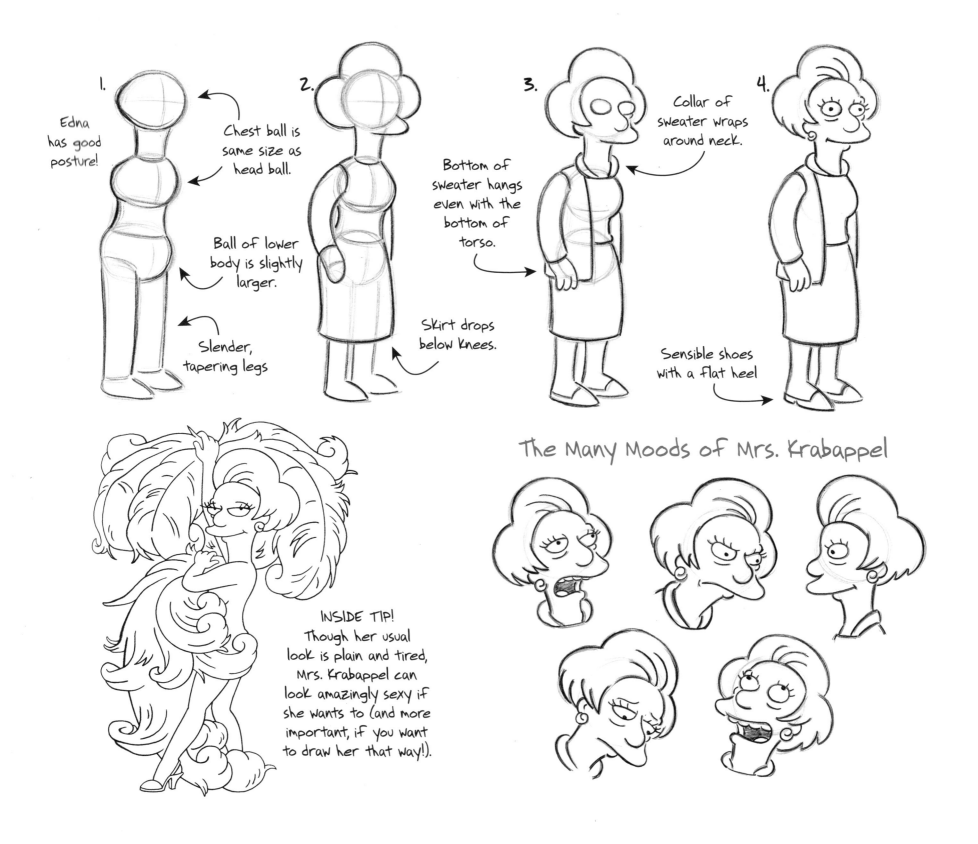

1. Edna has good posture!

Chest ball is same size as head ball.

Ball of lower body is slightly larger.

Slender, tapering legs

2. Skirt drops below knees.

3. Collar of sweater wraps around neck.

Bottom of sweater hangs even with the bottom of torso.

4. Sensible shoes with a flat heel

The Many Moods of Mrs. Krabappel

INSIDE TIP!
Though her usual look is plain and tired, Mrs. Krabappel can look amazingly sexy if she wants to (and more important, if you want to draw her that way!).

SIDESHOW BOB

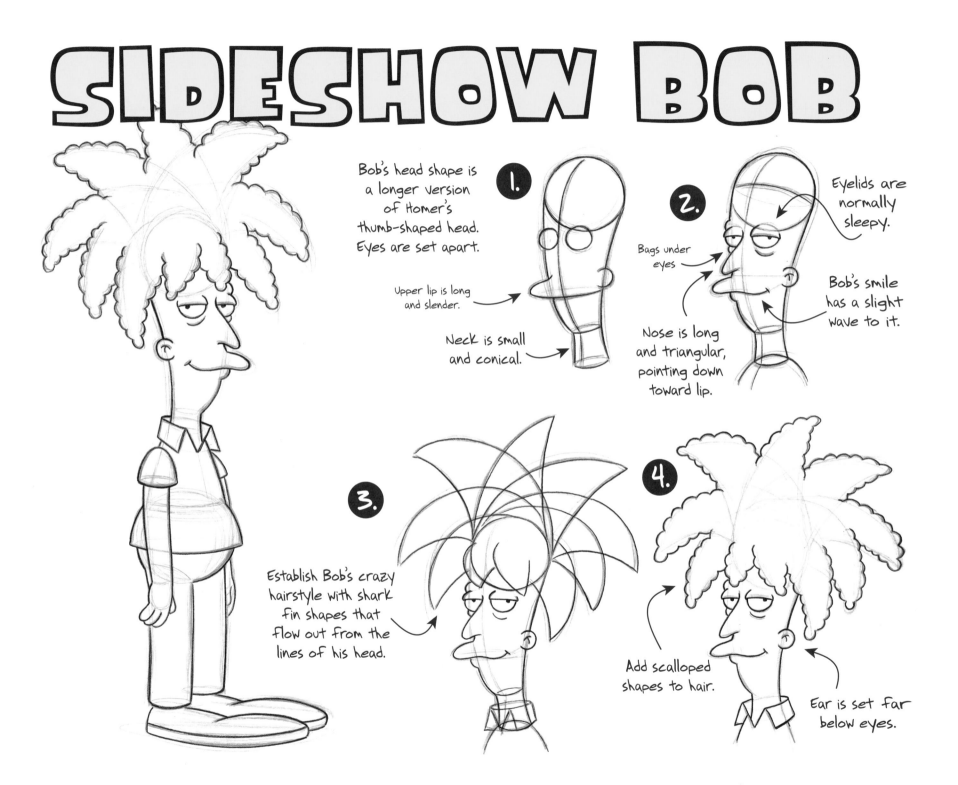

Bob's head shape is a longer version of Homer's thumb-shaped head. Eyes are set apart.

Upper lip is long and slender.

Neck is small and conical.

1.

2.

Eyelids are normally sleepy.

Bags under eyes

Bob's smile has a slight wave to it.

Nose is long and triangular, pointing down toward lip.

3.

Establish Bob's crazy hairstyle with shark fin shapes that flow out from the lines of his head.

4.

Add scalloped shapes to hair.

Ear is set far below eyes.

1. Torso is similar to Bart's in size and shape.

Because of his unusually long head, Bob is roughly 2 1/2 heads tall.

Legs are long and slender.

2. Feet are incredibly long.

3. Shirt collar sits low on neck, well away from his chin.

Slender arms hang low on shoulder.

4. Shirt is similar to Homer's.

INSIDE TIP! When drawing Bob's head and hair, think of a palm tree!

The Many Maniacal Moods of Sideshow Bob

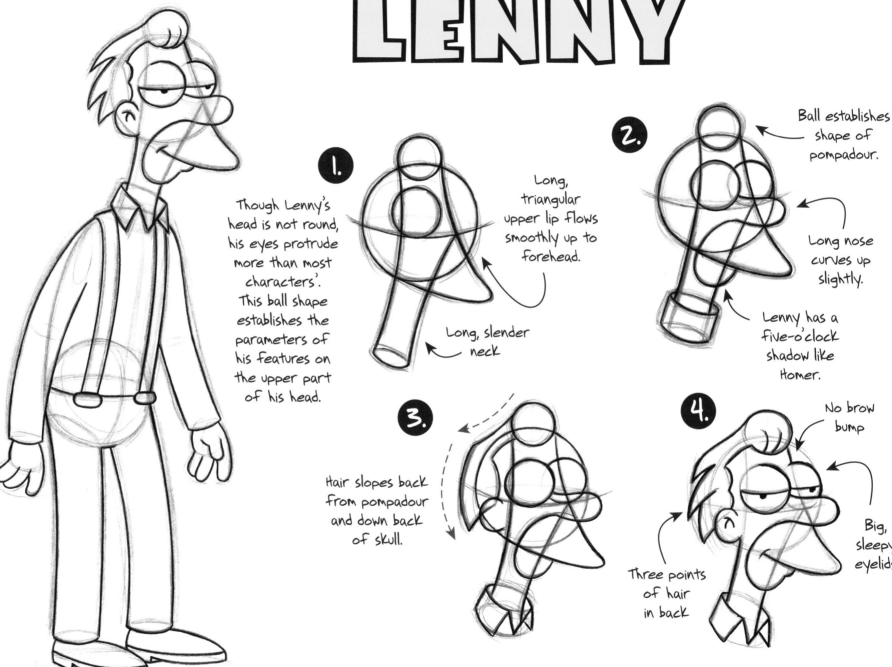

LENNY

1. Though Lenny's head is not round, his eyes protrude more than most characters'. This ball shape establishes the parameters of his features on the upper part of his head.

Long, triangular upper lip flows smoothly up to forehead.

Long, slender neck

2. Ball establishes shape of pompadour.

Long nose curves up slightly.

Lenny has a five-o'clock shadow like Homer.

3. Hair slopes back from pompadour and down back of skull.

4. No brow bump

Three points of hair in back

Big, sleepy eyelids

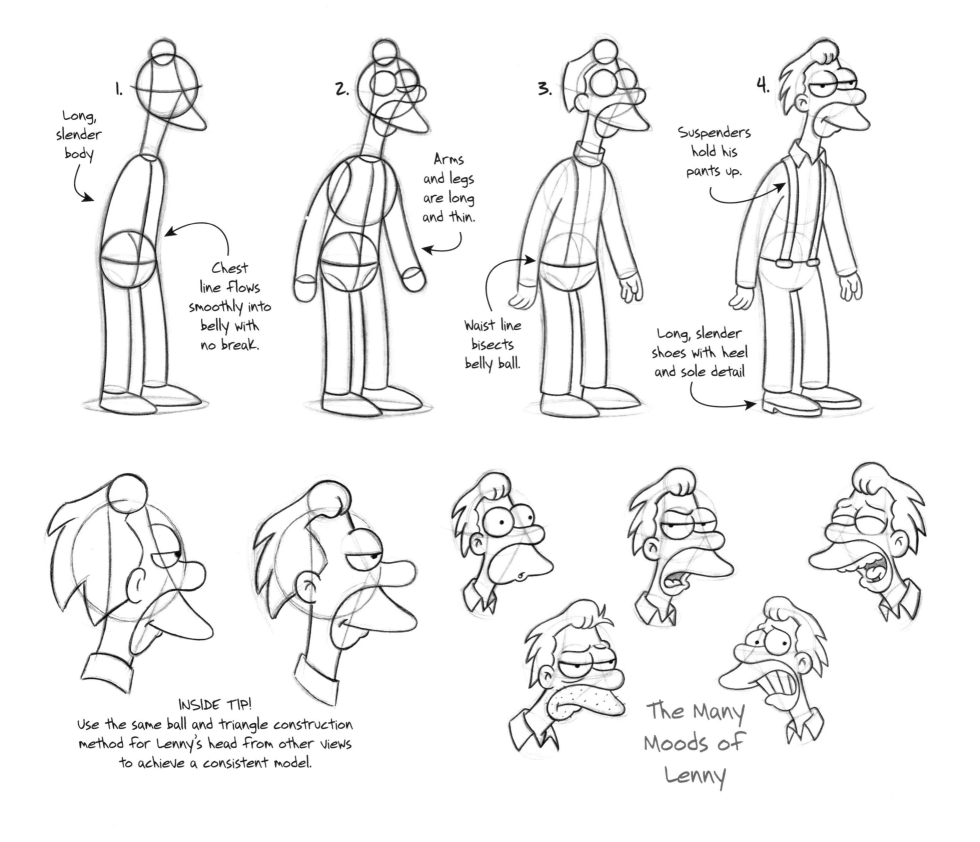

1. Long, slender body

Chest line flows smoothly into belly with no break.

2. Arms and legs are long and thin.

3. Waist line bisects belly ball.

4. Suspenders hold his pants up.

Long, slender shoes with heel and sole detail

INSIDE TIP!
Use the same ball and triangle construction method for Lenny's head from other views to achieve a consistent model.

The Many Moods of Lenny

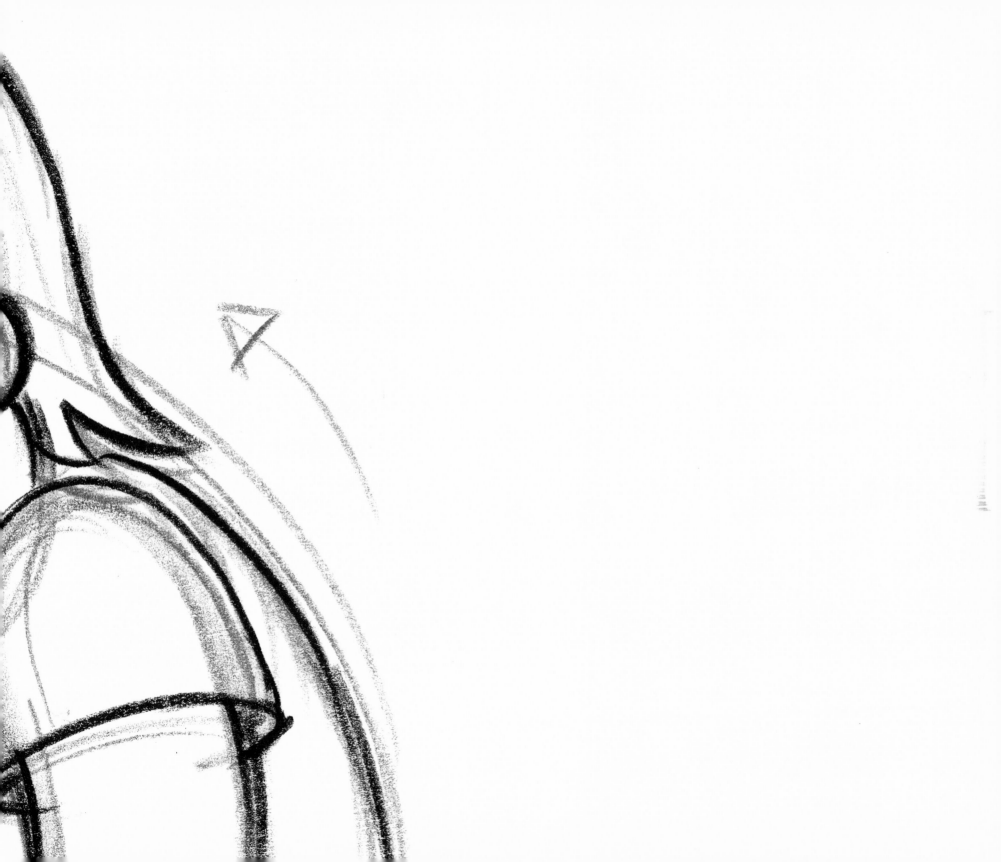

CARL

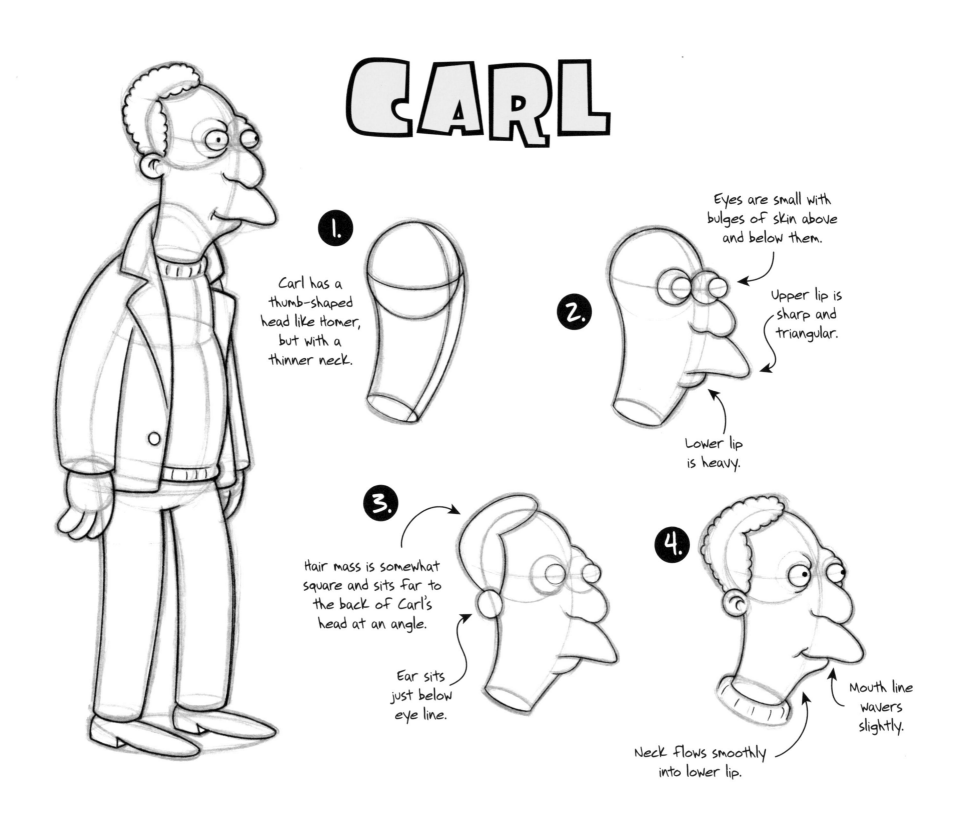

1. Carl has a thumb-shaped head like Homer, but with a thinner neck.

2. Eyes are small with bulges of skin above and below them.

Upper lip is sharp and triangular.

Lower lip is heavy.

3. Hair mass is somewhat square and sits far to the back of Carl's head at an angle.

Ear sits just below eye line.

4. Mouth line wavers slightly.

Neck flows smoothly into lower lip.

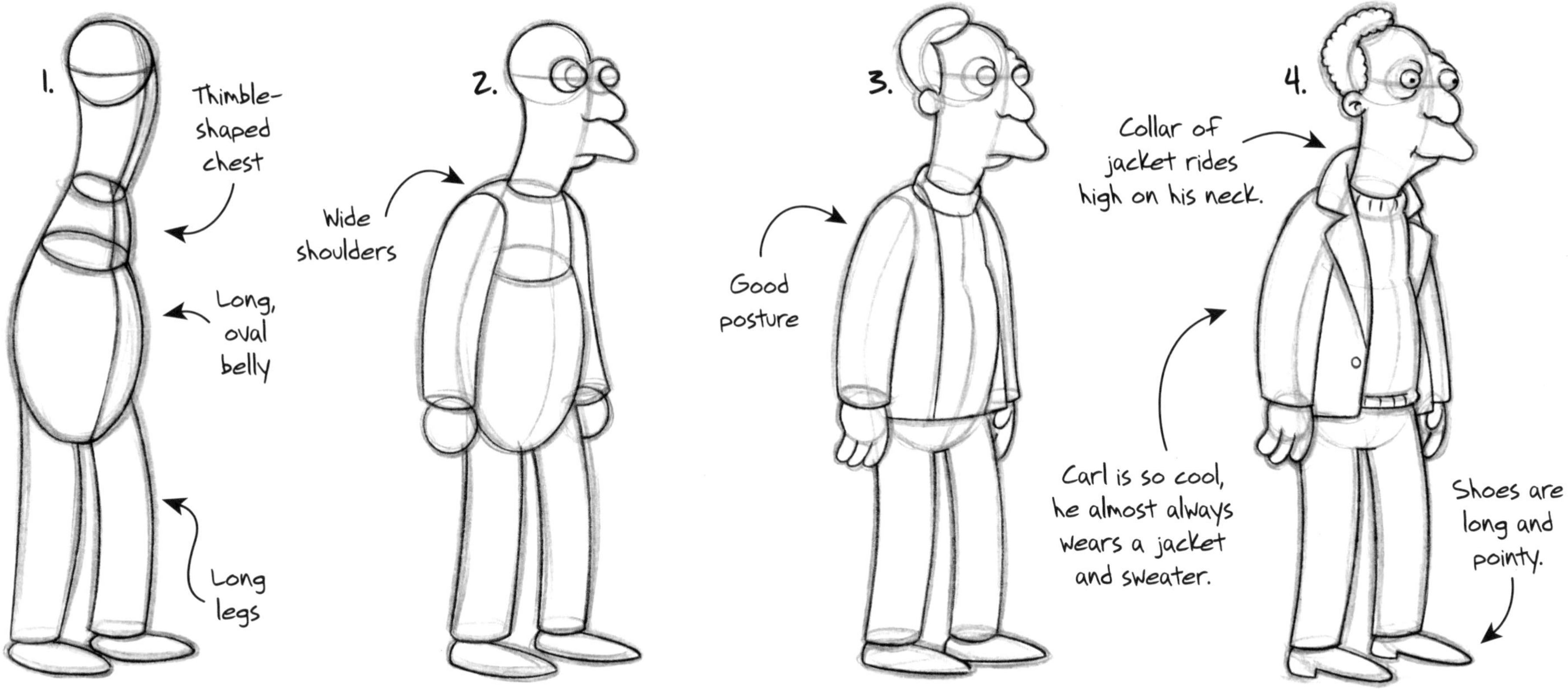

1. Thimble-shaped chest

Long, oval belly

Long legs

2. Wide shoulders

3. Good posture

Carl is so cool, he almost always wears a jacket and sweater.

4. Collar of jacket rides high on his neck.

Shoes are long and pointy.

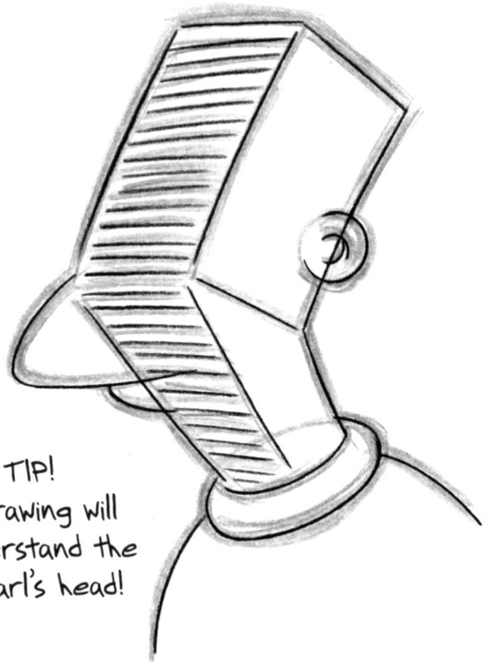

INSIDE TIP!
This cubic drawing will help you understand the angles of Carl's head!

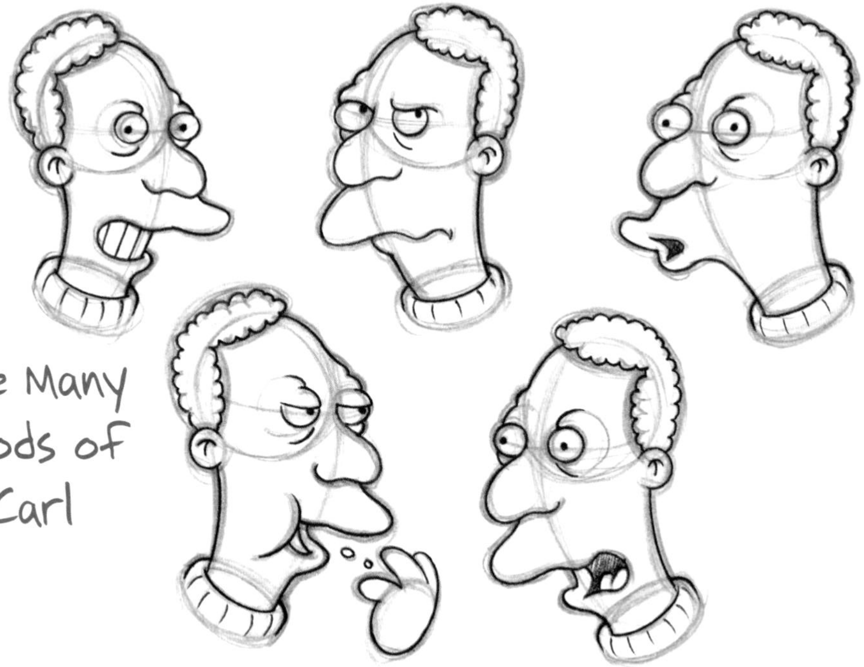

The Many Moods of Carl

NED FLANDERS

1. Ned has a ball-shaped head on a slightly conical neck.

2. Facial features are similar to the Simpson's family. (Could they be related?)

3. Full head of hair wraps neatly around head and hangs down below ear. Don't forget the stem of his glasses.

Mustache shape is like the upper third of a circle and overlaps the upper lip.

Hair wraps around forehead.

4. Lines in hair curve up and back.

Smile peeks out from behind mustache.

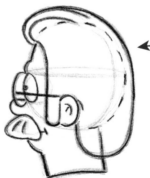

Ned's hair should be treated as a solid helmet-like mass.

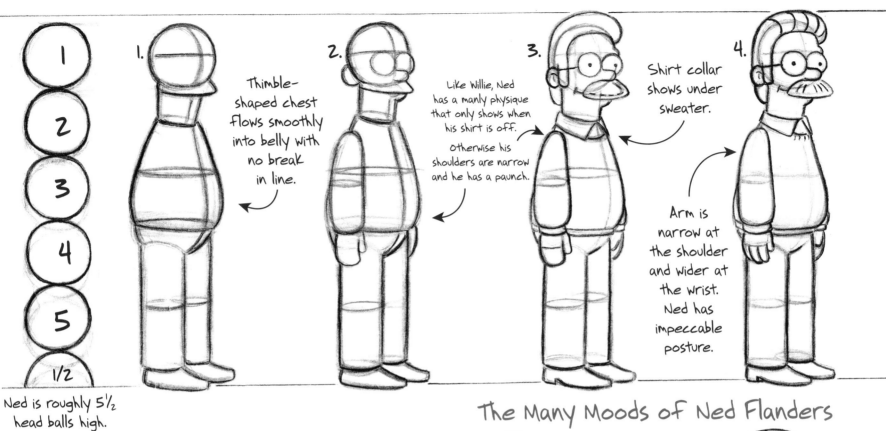

1 2 3 4 5 1/2

Ned is roughly 5½ head balls high.

1.

Thimble-shaped chest flows smoothly into belly with no break in line.

2.

Like Willie, Ned has a manly physique that only shows when his shirt is off.

Otherwise his shoulders are narrow and he has a paunch.

3.

Shirt collar shows under sweater.

4.

Arm is narrow at the shoulder and wider at the wrist. Ned has impeccable posture.

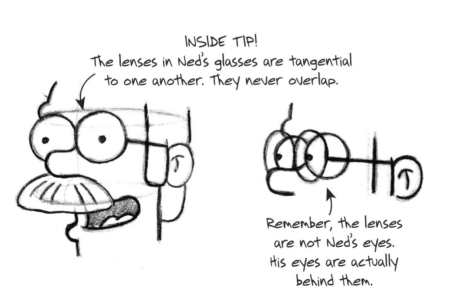

INSIDE TIP!
The lenses in Ned's glasses are tangential to one another. They never overlap.

Remember, the lenses are not Ned's eyes. His eyes are actually behind them.

The Many Moods of Ned Flanders

RALPH WIGGUM

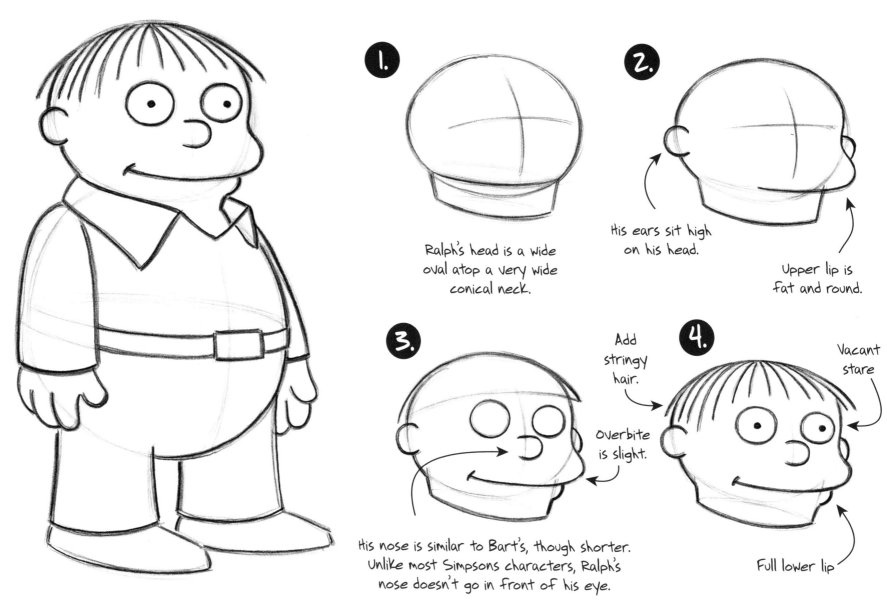

1. Ralph's head is a wide oval atop a very wide conical neck.

2. His ears sit high on his head.

Upper lip is fat and round.

3. His nose is similar to Bart's, though shorter. Unlike most Simpsons characters, Ralph's nose doesn't go in front of his eye.

Overbite is slight.

Add stringy hair.

4. Vacant stare

Full lower lip

Ralph's posture is very straight.

1.

Body is a large, vertical oval shape.

Legs are wide and set apart.

2.

Ralph's arms are wide and short.

Shirt tucks into pants.

Feet are long and narrow.

3.

Shirt has a wide collar and long sleeves.

Belt

4.

Waistline is high.

Ralph has fat, stubby fingers.

Add belt buckle.

INSIDE TIP!
Always draw a curving horizontal line across Ralph's forehead to establish his signature bowl-cut hairstyle!

The Many Moods of Ralph Wiggum

MOE

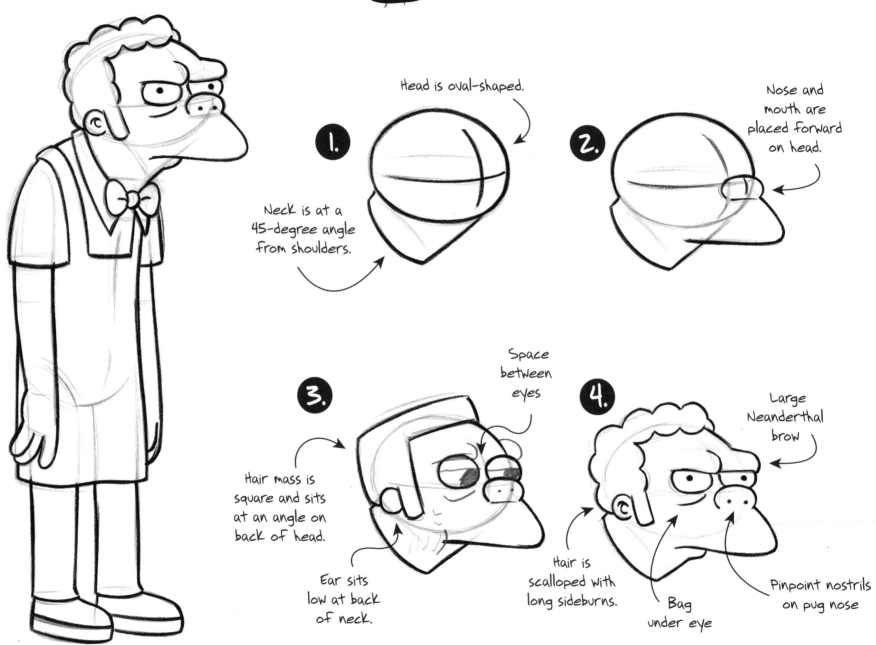

1. Head is oval-shaped.

Neck is at a 45-degree angle from shoulders.

2. Nose and mouth are placed forward on head.

3. Hair mass is square and sits at an angle on back of head.

Space between eyes

Ear sits low at back of neck.

4. Large Neanderthal brow

Hair is scalloped with long sideburns.

Bag under eye

Pinpoint nostrils on pug nose

1.

Thick neck

Long legs

Long, skinny body

2.

Slouched posture

Arms hang low on shoulder.

Smallish feet

Short sleeves are unusually long.

Chest line flows smoothly into belly with no break.

3.

Long, slender collar and bow tie.

Apron hangs just above knee line.

4.

Note how head hangs way over feet.

INSIDE TIP!
Moe has seven scallops of hair on the top and back, and five around his face (only four when in profile as he is here). They are uneven in size, giving him an unruly look!

The Many Moods of Moe

COMIC BOOK GUY

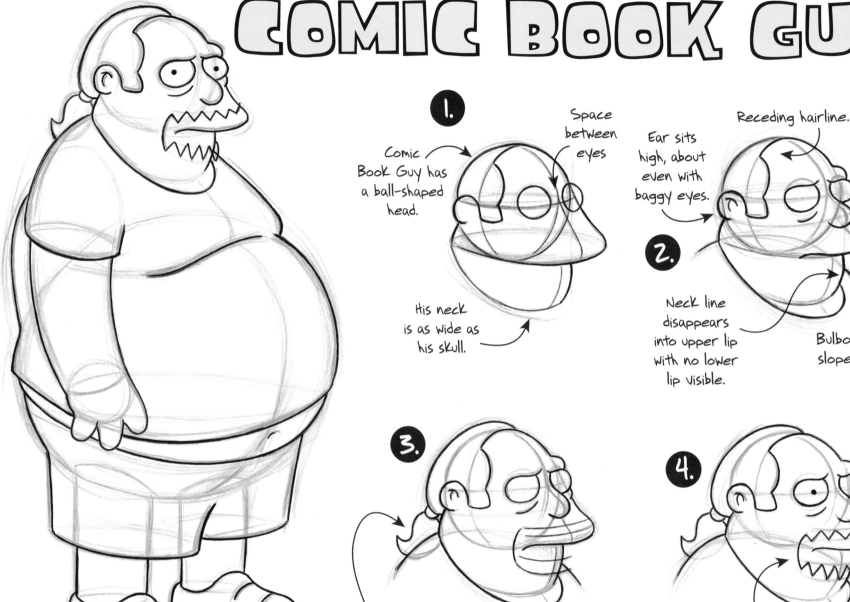

1.

Comic Book Guy has a ball-shaped head.

Space between eyes

His neck is as wide as his skull.

2.

Ear sits high, about even with baggy eyes.

Receding hairline.

Neck line disappears into upper lip with no lower lip visible.

Bulbous nose slopes down.

3.

Hair flows back away from skull and gathers into a ponytail.

4.

Beard line is suggested by a jagged line similar to the hair that wraps around Homer's head.

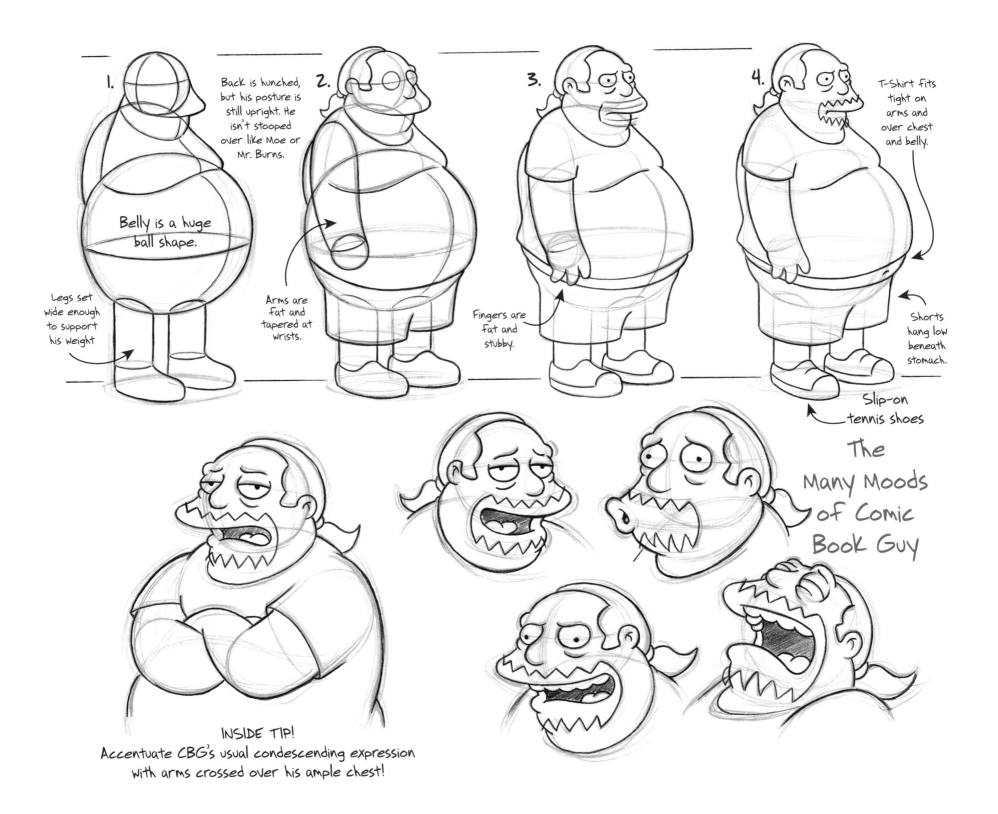

1.

Back is hunched, but his posture is still upright. He isn't stooped over like Moe or Mr. Burns.

Belly is a huge ball shape.

Legs set wide enough to support his weight

2.

Arms are fat and tapered at wrists.

3.

Fingers are fat and stubby.

4.

T-Shirt fits tight on arms and over chest and belly.

Shorts hang low beneath stomach.

Slip-on tennis shoes

The Many Moods of Comic Book Guy

INSIDE TIP!
Accentuate CBG's usual condescending expression with arms crossed over his ample chest!

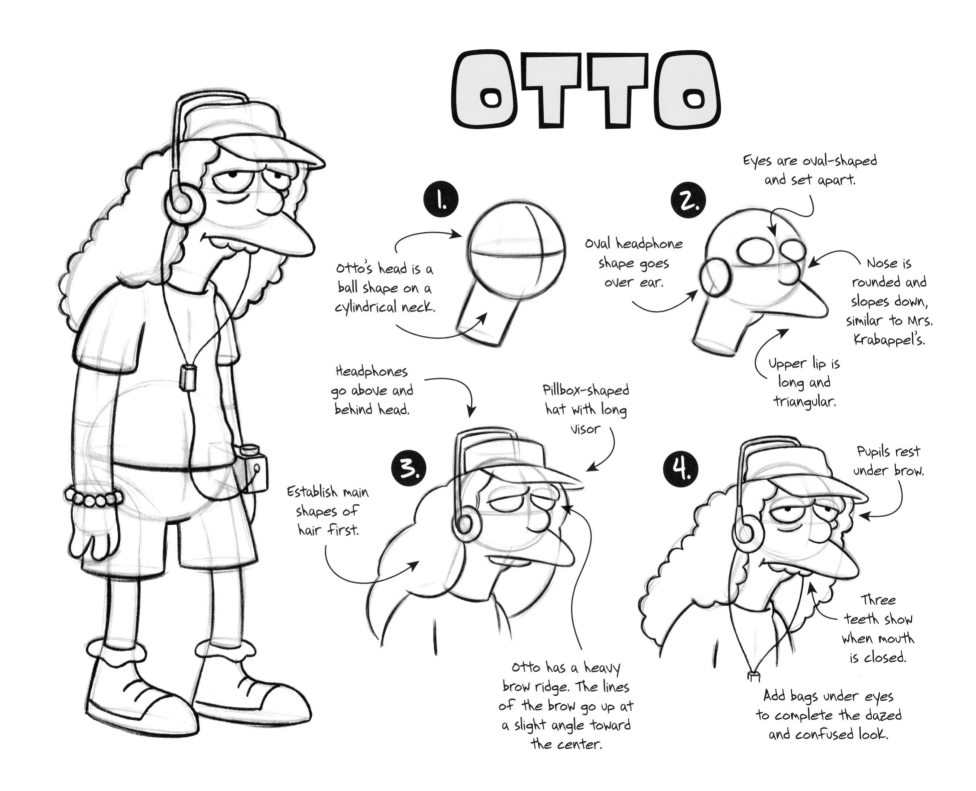

OTTO

1. Otto's head is a ball shape on a cylindrical neck.

2. Oval headphone shape goes over ear.

Eyes are oval-shaped and set apart.

Nose is rounded and slopes down, similar to Mrs. Krabappel's.

Upper lip is long and triangular.

Headphones go above and behind head.

Pillbox-shaped hat with long visor

3. Establish main shapes of hair first.

Otto has a heavy brow ridge. The lines of the brow go up at a slight angle toward the center.

4. Pupils rest under brow.

Three teeth show when mouth is closed.

Add bags under eyes to complete the dazed and confused look.

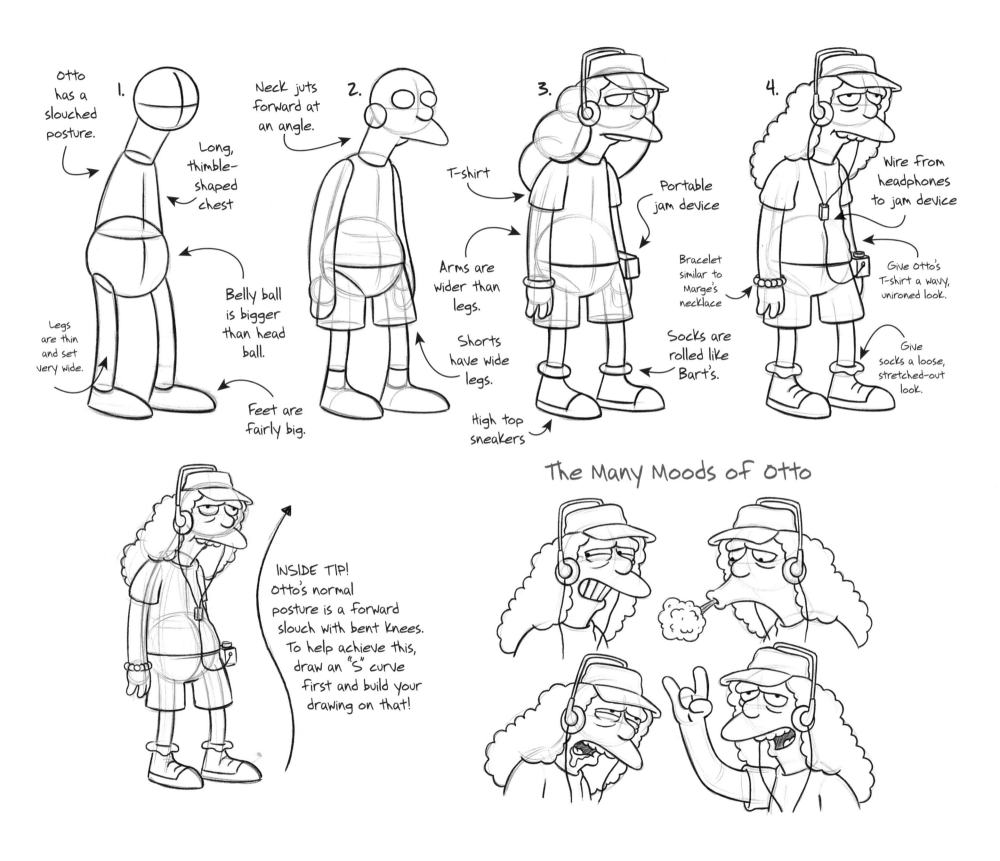

Otto has a slouched posture.

1.

Long, thimble-shaped chest

Legs are thin and set very wide.

Belly ball is bigger than head ball.

Feet are fairly big.

2.

Neck juts forward at an angle.

Arms are wider than legs.

Shorts have wide legs.

3.

T-shirt

Portable jam device

Bracelet similar to Marge's necklace

Socks are rolled like Bart's.

High top sneakers

4.

Wire from headphones to jam device

Give Otto's T-shirt a wavy, unironed look.

Give socks a loose, stretched-out look.

INSIDE TIP! Otto's normal posture is a forward slouch with bent knees. To help achieve this, draw an "S" curve first and build your drawing on that!

The Many Moods of Otto

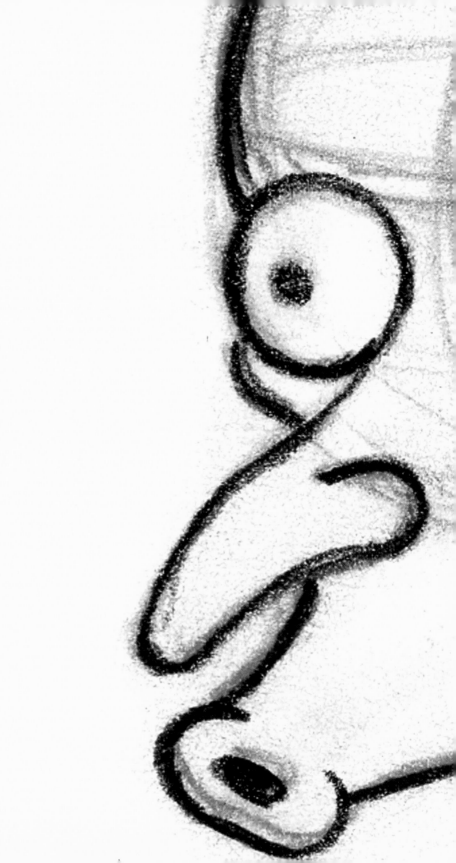

SANTA'S LITTLE HELPER AND SNOWBALL II

2. Use converging lines to establish shape of ears and fur tufts.

1. Snowball II has a wide oval head on a conical neck.

Eyes are oval and set apart.

Oval nose sits below eyes.

Long, triangular upper lip

Long, narrow pupils

Collar wraps around base of neck.

3. Define triangular ears and fur tufts.

Two whiskers

Sharp teeth

Triangular ears sit high and back on head.

1. Santa's Little Helper has a ball-shaped head on a conical neck.

Eye is above center line of head.

2.

Wall-eyed gaze

Oval-shaped nose at tip of snout

3.

Snout is long and triangular.

1.

Curvy "S" shapes help establish the form.

2.

3.

Don't forget to add the three rib lines.

Santa's Little Helper is a greyhound. He has a long oval chest that tapers down to a slender abdomen, and thin, yet muscular, legs.

1.

2.

"S" shaped tail

3.

4.

Snowball II has a long, capsule-shaped body on short, cylindrical legs.

Head juts out at a 45-degree angle from body.

Though haunches aren't seen in this standing pose, they are evident when you see Snowball II sitting, running, etc.

INSIDE TIP!
Of course, you can show different expressions on Santa's Little Helper by changing his eyes and mouth, but you can also use his ears!

The Many Moods of The Simpsons' Pets

ITCHY & SCRATCHY

Itchy has disk-shaped ears.

Both Itchy and Scratchy have ball-shaped heads.

1.

Scratchy has shark fin-shaped ears.

Itchy's upper lip is long and triangular.

Scratchy's upper lip is more oval-shaped.

Itchy has round, overlapping eyes and an oval nose.

2.

Scratchy's eyes are round and set apart. His nose is a rounded triangle.

3. Block in fur shapes.

Add cleavage to Scratchy's upper lip.

Scratchy has three tufts of hair on top and three at the back of his head.

Itchy has three tufts of fur on his forehead and one at the back of his head.

4.

Two bucked teeth

Two fangs

Tongue is usually sticking out.

1. Scratchy has a long body with a slouched posture.

Itchy has a short upper body and long legs.

Head and belly balls are roughly the same size on both Itchy and Scratchy.

2. Tubular arms

Add Itchy's vest!

Don't forget the tails!

3. Both have oval fur patches on their upper bodies.

Give them white gloves.

Both have belly buttons.

Feet are pawlike with three toes each.

The Malevolent Mayhem of Itchy and Scratchy

FUN FACT!
Itchy and Scratchy's white gloves are based on those of many classic cartoon characters of the 1930s and 1940s!

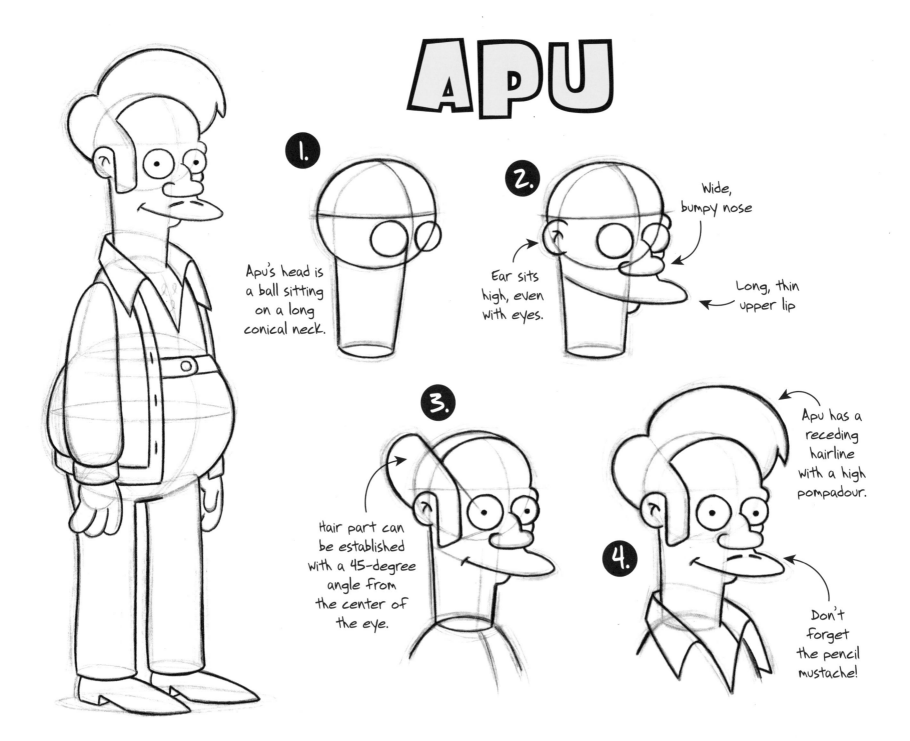

APU

1. Apu's head is a ball sitting on a long conical neck.

2. Wide, bumpy nose

Ear sits high, even with eyes.

Long, thin upper lip

3. Hair part can be established with a 45-degree angle from the center of the eye.

4. Apu has a receding hairline with a high pompadour.

Don't forget the pencil mustache!

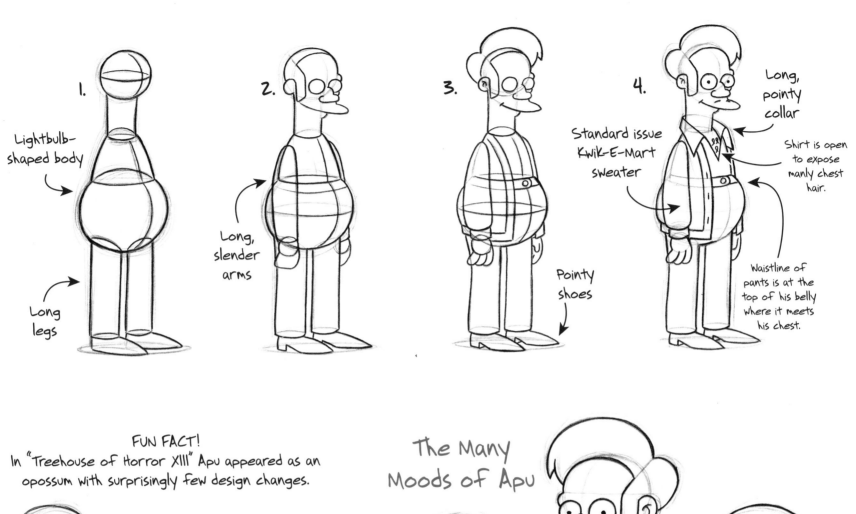

1.

Lightbulb-shaped body

Long legs

2.

Long, slender arms

3.

Pointy shoes

4.

Standard issue Kwik-E-Mart sweater

Long, pointy collar

Shirt is open to expose manly chest hair.

Waistline of pants is at the top of his belly where it meets his chest.

FUN FACT!

In "Treehouse of Horror XIII" Apu appeared as an opossum with surprisingly few design changes.

The Many Moods of Apu

PRINCIPAL SKINNER

1. Skinner's head is a standard ball shape on a wide, slightly conical neck.

2. Ear is peanut-shaped.

Eyes are smallish and set apart.

Triangular nose points down to triangular upper lip.

3. Block in unruly hair shape first.

Thick lower lip

4. Cowlick with 3 sharp points of hair

Brow line

Jowl line

Bags under eyes

1. Skinner has wide, square shoulders.

Long upper body

Short legs

2. Arms hang low off the shoulders, leaving room for the collar of his jacket.

Smallish feet

3. Wide lapels

Wide tie

Bottom of jacket is slightly scalloped.

4. Sensible shoes

INSIDE TIP! Skinner's hair can be tough to draw. Sketch in a square at an angle off the ball of his skull, and then round it off. This will help establish the basic shape!

The Many Moods of Principal Skinner

PATTY AND SELMA

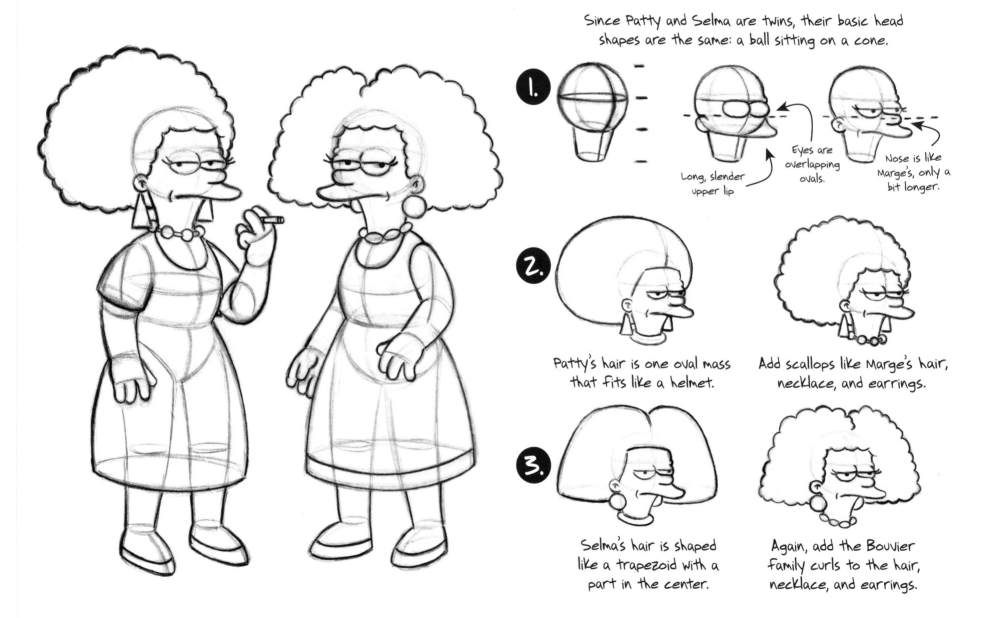

Since Patty and Selma are twins, their basic head shapes are the same: a ball sitting on a cone.

1.

Long, slender upper lip

Eyes are overlapping ovals.

Nose is like Marge's, only a bit longer.

2.

Patty's hair is one oval mass that fits like a helmet.

Add scallops like Marge's hair, necklace, and earrings.

3.

Selma's hair is shaped like a trapezoid with a part in the center.

Again, add the Bouvier family curls to the hair, necklace, and earrings.

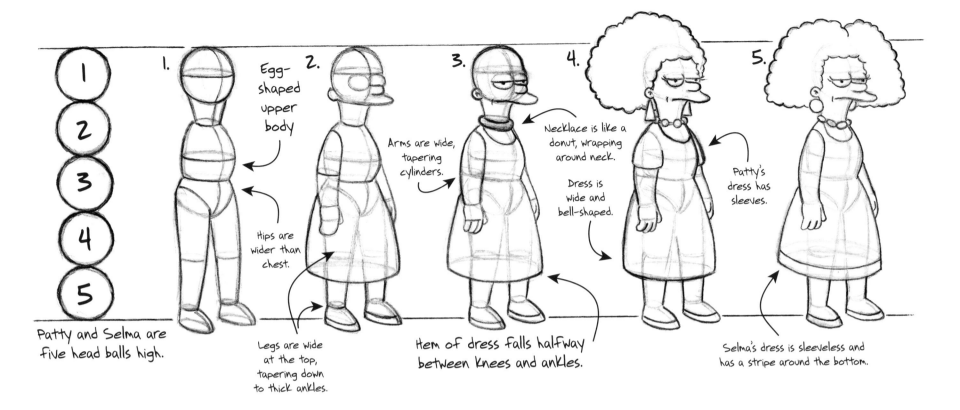

1 2 3 4 5

Patty and Selma are five head balls high.

1.

Egg-shaped upper body

Hips are wider than chest.

2.

Arms are wide, tapering cylinders.

Legs are wide at the top, tapering down to thick ankles.

3.

Hem of dress falls halfway between knees and ankles.

4.

Necklace is like a donut, wrapping around neck.

Dress is wide and bell-shaped.

5.

Patty's dress has sleeves.

Selma's dress is sleeveless and has a stripe around the bottom.

INSIDE TIP!

Patty and Selma have slightly different tastes in jewelry, another way to tell them apart! Patty has long triangular earrings. Selma has big round ones that hang below her ear from invisible hooks.

Patty's necklace is a series of small balls connected by a visible string that runs through them. Selma's necklace is a series of oval shapes that attach to each other.

The Many Moods of Patty and Selma

Now that you've learned to draw the
Simpson family and some of their fellow Springfieldians,
you'll want to be able to depict them interacting with each other.
At this point you may be asking, "How tall is Milhouse compared
to Bart? Is Kang shorter than Homer?" Here is a handy

SIZE-RELATIONSHIP CHART

to help you answer those questions for yourself!

Homer

Marge

Bart

Lisa

Maggie

Santas
Little
Helper

Snowball
2

Ralph

MILLHOUSE

Nelson

COSTUME CHANGES

Although the Simpsons characters usually wear the same clothes, they occasionally change into other duds as the situation dictates. Here are several typical costume changes for various characters.

SLEEPWEAR

VACATION WEAR

WINTER WEAR

REAL
ESTATE
AGENT

COUCH
POTATO

SUNDAY
BEST

SATURDAY
WORST

RACE
CAR DRIVER

ASTRONAUT

DANCIN'
HOMER

CUPCAKE KID

PIE MAN

MONORAIL
CONDUCTOR

FOOL

LUCKY RED HAT

DIAPER

BARTMAN

HIPPIE KID

SUNDAY BEST

HOCKEY

SUNDAY BEST

BACKGROUNDS AND PROPS

THE SIMPSONS' KITCHEN

Let's talk about backgrounds. They may not be quite as important as the characters, and you may never see a T-shirt featuring Marge's corncob curtains, but let's face it, without backgrounds the characters would flounder in an empty void.

Observational details are key elements of every Simpsons background drawing. In these kitchen views, notice that even though the lines are simplified to work well with the style of the characters, they still give the impression of being real spaces. The perspectives aren't skewed, and the elements aren't drawn in a "cartoony" way. It's all based on real objects and real architecture.

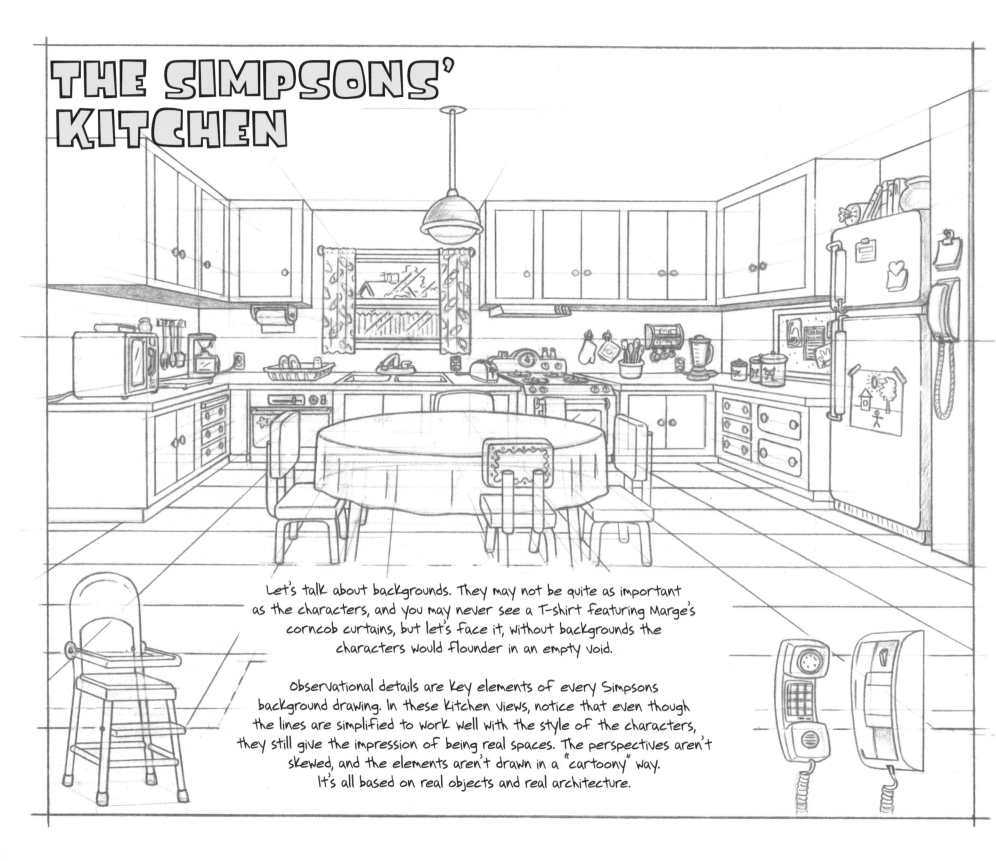

Notice how the details of the backgrounds tell you things about the characters. The drawing taped to the fridge tells you that Marge and Homer are proud parents. The stool in the corner reminds you that Bart needs to take a time-out every once in a while. The crack in the wall is evidence that Homer spends more time watching TV than doing home repairs.

These things may seem insignificant, but they help create the illusion that the Simpsons are real characters existing in a real universe.

THE SIMPSONS' TV ROOM

Notice the light perspective lines in these views of the TV room, all going to single vanishing points in the center of the drawings. This is known as "one-point perspective." As the viewer, this perspective places us in the center of the room at about eye level with the vanishing point. The angle at which we see all of the elements in the room is based on that one-point perspective.

For example, if we were able to see
the top of Homer's stereo, even though we can't
see the top of the shelf it's sitting on, the stereo would be
out of perspective or not in correct relationship with the
vanishing point. Note that we CAN see the tops of the
stereo speakers. That's because they are below the
vanishing point and, thus, below our eye line.

MOE'S TAVERN

Can you tell what perspective was used to create this drawing? If you said "one-point," reward yourself with a tall, cool Duff (or a pickled egg if you're underage!).

The vanishing point is just to the left of the door. Notice how the lines of the floor, ceiling, pool table, bar, etc., all go to that point. Now check out the TV. You can tell that it's hanging off the wall at an odd angle because the lines don't relate at all to the vanishing point.

The pencil shading here further helps to illustrate that the elements in this drawing are based on observing real objects. Everything in the room has convincing form, shape, weight, and detail.

THE ANDROID'S DUNGEON

Speaking of detail, this sketch takes the cake! Simpsons background designer Lance Wilder has obviously been to a comic book store or two in his day. The observational details are so convincing you can almost smell the moldy paper and greasy onion rings.

The dotted lines indicate placement of elements like a comic book rack (in the center of the floor) and other display fixtures that have been removed to allow us a better view.

THE KWIK-E-MART

These views of Apu's retail establishment are drawn in a
"two-point perspective." In the case of the first view, we the
viewers are at a vantage point looking down on the room. We can tell
that our eye line is above the top of the Squishee machine because
we can just barely see its top surface. Notice how the lines of
the floor, magazines, countertops, etc., all go to points
on the eye line (or horizon line) outside the drawing
on both the right and the left sides.

The two-point perspective allows us to see the room at an odd angle. We're not in the center of the room as we were in the Simpsons' TV room. Now we're off to the side and we can see two sides of most of the elements in the room. However, if we were standing directly facing, say, the Squishee machine, our perspective would change to one-point and we would see only the machine's back surface.

BART'S CLASSROOM

Here's a rare example of "three-point perspective."
We're obviously looking down on the room from such a height that the horizon line is well off the page. This bird's-eye view is what also creates the third point in what would otherwise be two-point perspective.
You can follow the horizontal lines of the classroom door, the bookshelves, the sides of the desks, and the windows to the first vanishing point off the top of the page. The lines of the fronts and backs of the desks go to the second vanishing point off to the right of the page. The third vanishing point is off the bottom of the page. Notice how the classroom door is wider at the top than it is at the bottom? Normally the vertical lines of the door would be parallel to each other, but because our vantage point is so high, those lines also recede into perspective. All the vertical lines in this drawing go to the third vanishing point.

LEARN PERSPECTIVE
LEARN PERSPECTIVE
LEARN PERSPECTIVE
LEARN PERSPECTIVE
LEARN PERSPECTIVE

THE KRUSTY THE CLOWN SHOW SET

This drawing is a tricky one. Because of the circular center ring area and bleacher placement, there are lots of perspectives going on here. The cameras, lights, props, and Applause signs are all at odd angles to each other and to the general perspective of the room. However, it's a very organized chaos. The floor lines, ceiling lines, and proscenium arch are actually in a one-point perspective. Many of the other elements have a two-point perspective because they are not at right angles with the rest of the room. Yet, everything works together to make one believable and fantastic drawing!

HOMER'S WORK STATION

Most of us don't know what the inside of an actual nuclear power plant looks like, but these views of Homer's work station are pretty convincing. We don't know what most of these dials, knobs, and switches do, but neither does Homer.

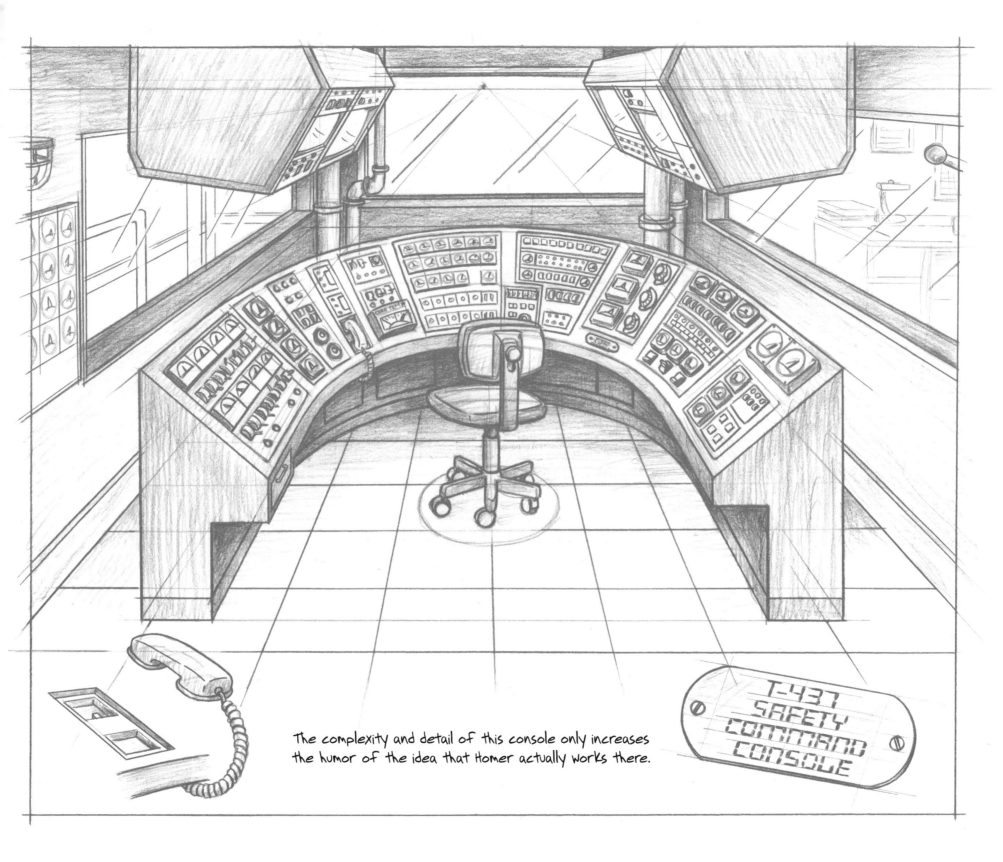

The complexity and detail of this console only increases
the humor of the idea that Homer actually works there.

T-437
SAFETY
COMMAND
CONSOLE

When it comes to "The Simpsons," idle hands are the cartoonist's playground.
Here are a couple of pages of props to give those hands something to do. Like the backgrounds,
the props in the Simpsons universe are very observational. They have a very hand-drawn, organic look, yet,
as you can see by the shading on these preliminary sketches, their design comes from observing real objects.
For comparison, a few of the preliminary sketches are shown with their final animation line counterparts.

All the individual aspects of drawing that we've examined are essential to building a scene with characters interacting in a setting. Whether your goal is creating an animated cartoon, a comic book, or an illustration, sooner or later you have to bring all the elements together. So why wait? Let's do it now!

The opposite page with overlays illustrates the evolution of a scene from its rough, block-shape layout stage, to a rough pencil sketch, followed by a tight pencil drawing, and ending with the final ink line illustration in full color! Study them well and use them as a guide to build your own cartoon masterpieces!